NEW POETRY
FROM THE
MIDWEST
2019

2019 HEARTLAND POETRY PRIZE WINNERS

"Hometown Nocturne"

by Leila Chatti

"Cock Fight"

by Christopher Nelson

"Practice"

by Kimberly Ann Priest

NEW POETRY FROM THE MIDWEST

2019

RITA MAE REESE & HANNAH STEPHENSON
Series Editors

WILLIAM EVANS
Judge of the 2019 Heartland Poetry Prizes

newamericanpress
Milwaukee, Wis

n e w a m e r i c a n p r e s s

www.NewAmericanPress.com

Printed in the United States of America

Interior design by Abigail Archer
Cover design by Brian Maztat

Cover image by Steve Halama on Unsplash
www.unsplash.com

ISBN 9781941561201

For ordering information, please contact:
Ingram Book Group
One Ingram Blvd.
La Vergne, TN 37086
(800) 937-8000
orders@ingrambook.com

TABLE OF CONTENTS

EDITORS' NOTE

When you say or hear "Midwest," you likely conjure up images of straight roads through cornfields and lonesome farm houses. Maybe you think "flyover country" without quite being able to help yourself, or maybe you think of Chicago or Detroit or the Rust Belt. So when you hear "Midwest poetry," you might think of straight lines between corn fields or skyscrapers or urban blight.

Every submission we received shows that assumption to be terribly wrong. The poems gathered here, from the hundreds of submissions we received, are filled with surprising turns, zigzagging through humor, pain, hope, fear, and loss. They are devastating, feverish, wry, fantastic, formal, and informal.

Roy Guzmán's poem "Blood Fantasia"—which is a loose-sestina cento that uses lines from poetry, novels, and interviews—inspired us to introduce you to the poets in this volume with a cento of our own.

The Midwest: A Cento

By June, I was still already grieving. [1]
how do we take off our bodies? [2]
"That's the kind of proof I like, a scar I can put [3]
in a graveyard. Another labors along the length of a canyon. [4]
I tell you a story about the lobster? When the lobster grows, [5]
her despair. For becoming forest and for deforestation. For [6]
The other night I was walking home and I got viciously scared. [7]
It's the garden spider who eats her mistakes [8]

---

[1] "Late Summer," Derrick Austin

[2] "Elegy for What Almost Was," Rebekah Hewitt

[3] "The Ruts," Kim Lozana

[4] "Phantom Routes," Matthew Olzmann

[5] "When the Lobster Grows," Joshua Lefkowitz

[6] "D," Claire Wahmanholm

[7] "Polyphonic Autopsy of a Woman Who May Not andor Cannot Exist," Joy Belonger

[8] "Oh Wonder," Traci Brimhall

bullet / down the esophagus / [9]
The wheel is broken behind her, [10]
She thinks about all the mirrors in the houses [11]
Right here weary world I park the flashbacks [12]
souvenirs—our songs, the memories we don't want, [13]
tongues of flame, cheap bulbs burning in fir branches, [14]
cigarettes, kisses, a knife in a cake. [15]
If we believe what God says about Adam: [16]
This place in which I dream the new body—whole and abiding— [17]

This year's anthology features many, many new voices, as well as some
that might be familiar to you from the two previous volumes of *New
Poetry from the Midwest* (published in 2014 and 2017). But we are missing
the voice of Okla Elliott, who founded and co-edited this series prior to
his untimely passing in 2017. Though his voice is absent, his spirit and
influence are not. We dedicate this year's anthology to his memory, and
to the memory of other poets that we have lost this year.

— Rita Mae Reese and Hannah Stephenson
Series Editors

[9] "Feeding Cycle," Geramee Hensley

[10] "Breaking the Wheel," Lisa Ampleman

[11] "How Ella Knows," Jeffrey Bean

[12] "When We Sing of Might," Kimberly Blaeser

[13] "Carried," Andrew Collard

[14] "Hometown Nocturne," Leila Chatti

[15] "Going Deaf," Mary Brown

[16] "Six Reasons I Can't Answer the Door for Him at 3 in the Morning," Sarah Carson

[17] "On Visiting the Franklin Park Conservatory & Botanical Gardens," Khaty Xiong

INTRODUCTION

Please make no mistake, there were far more than these three poems that are worthy of distinction. This is an anthology after all, and you would strain yourself at the point of harm to find a poem in this collection that wasn't capable of captivating you. These three stood out to me however, in the clear voiced certainty of the writer and often uncertainty of the speaker that pulls you into the stanzas themselves.

What's intoxicating about "Hometown Nocturne" is the way the poem invites you into its world with open arms even while the speaker themselves is othered in this world. Everything in this poem has a texture, be it prickly or worn down to slick finish. The ending of this poem is a masterclass of tying a bow off on a piece without looking like you're tying a bow:

> I carved carefully my name in frost.
> Scuffed my feet the whole way home.
> The hooded eyes of houses
> looked on a past me. The huddled trees
> whispered, brandished pom-poms just for show.

"Practice" begins with a pretty high bar, and the images it continues to evoke are often staggering in their malice:

> Autumn. Leaves drip and turn over,
> round like the goblet of a thigh torn from its animal.

But even the captivating imagery doesn't rival the turn in this poem. The surprise and terror captured by the entrance of the children is haunting and brings the previous lines above sea level. There is a consequence to traveling inside of this poem, one the reader cannot passively dismiss.

A lot of poems use allegory to introduce their central themes, but they aren't always successful, leaving us to wonder what happened to the introductory image or what relevance it has on the poem. "Cock Fight" uses allegory successfully. The speaker is constantly beset with the hostile environment of the Colosseum. While this poem has the traits of a coming of age tale, the stakes are life and death for the speaker, often vacillating between memory and revelation. Dreamscape and a cold front. While there were many lines that struck me, this one left me breathless:

> ...In high school I had a secret lover.
> When he would enter me, what I marveled at most was how
>
> who I was—or thought I was—would fade,
> a much easier way to lose the self, I used to muse,
> than crawling for miles on the hands and knees,
> like pilgrims I read about, to a holy altar, where
> in the body's exhausted distress, what seems to be
>
> —and in fact may be—the soul leans outward, through the eyes...

What I loved about reading through this anthology was that it validates the pushback on those that think of the Midwest as a monolith. The space between the voices from our part of the country is rendered beautifully here, without compromise or apology. We speak on many things because we are many things. Few texts articulate that better than anthologies like this.

— William Evans
2019 Heartland Poetry Prize Judge

FOR OKLA

LISA AMPLEMAN

BREAKING THE WHEEL

As a child, I lived
    on St. Catherine Street,
        patron saint of unmarried girls

and knife sharpeners,
    spinsters and spinners.
        Strapped to a spiked wheel for torture

when she wouldn't
    consort with the emperor,
        she shattered it with her touch.

Impatient, the executioner
    took her head instead.
        At one end, St. Catherine Street

becomes Greengrass. In the middle,
    we sledded down the front-yard hill,
        whooping with joy or terror.

The street dead-ends
    near Coldwater Creek
        with its concrete banks and nuclear secrets:

runoff from radioactive waste
    leeched into its water
        decades ago. The kids who played

on its banks (my mother
      never let me) have
            salivary gland growths, thyroid tumors.

In one treatment, neutron therapy,
      the radiation takes away
            from what it gave.

In the room, a "vault,"
      photons bounce off a bit
            of beryllium, and the tumor's DNA

dances in the ray,
      cannot cope. The cell
            breaks, defeated wheel.

For years, the official word
      was: no link between
            their illness and the creek.

Now the state sifts the soil.
      Thorium lurks a few feet down.
            Don't breathe it in,

the researchers warn;
      no landscaping or tilling here.
            Use caution. We can clean this up.

Caravaggio's Catherine holds a sword,
>her dress sleeves white
>>against the dark shadows of her skirts.

The wheel is broken behind her,
>two spokes with empty couplings.
>>An unbroken halo curves

around her head, barely there,
>gold that might
>>float away on the lightest exhalation.

First published in *MIRACLE MONOCLE*

GEOFF ANDERSON

———

SKIN

I have never been able to decrypt
the melanin in me. The night I passed

into the earth, my father didn't care
how light I was. My mother tells me this

out of guilt I am so fair. In kindergarten,
I make a circle to draw her. To draw my father,

I fill one in. I am a ring with loops for hair,
my face the color of paper. Everything has a color.

5th St. black. Our roses white. Hair
pick black. Census black. Blue eyes white.

When I'm old enough to take notes,
my pen becomes a spade beneath my desk,

digging for roots in my skin, a blackness
temporary in the shower. It inks down

the vertebrae of the porcelain tub, my arms
bleached, my face a cloud of steam, no matter

how hard I wipe the mirror.

First published in PRETTY OWL POETRY

DERRICK AUSTIN

———

LATE SUMMER

By June, I was still already grieving.

Strobe lights swarmed over the dead in Orlando.
A cop executed Philando Castile in front of his beloved and her daughter;
Citizens shared the video like a chain letter.
I cloistered myself in grief. I did not shave. I ate bread and wine
And wine. Heard voices were my mother's calls.
I could not answer. I could not answer my phone. Was I an I?

The sky, a plum with a patch of gray rot. The wind, light.
A man I'd been fucking took me sailing on Lake Mendota.
We heard the disordered drums and yelps
Of someone who shouldn't sing marimba music
From the crescent of light where people caroused, forgot themselves.

He reached for my crotch, felt me harden.
I stopped desiring him months ago. My pleasure was in his not knowing.
And wanting me still. He returned me to simplicity, lust, selfishness
—Of the powers that separate us from animals, cruelty.

I thought there was salt in the air.
The scent of the Gulf that claims me,
Where I knew my people and myself.

Blue algae's been bad lately,
he said. *It's rot you're smelling.*

It's where the living's done.

First published in *PUERTO DEL SOL*

HOW ELLA KNOWS

Ella's hands know she's alive today.
Her piano is drenched in sunlight,

and she spends the morning coaxing hums
from its belly. She has made a pet of the wind,

and she lets it in through the screen door, feeds it
dried blooms from a rhododendron.

She thinks about all the mirrors in the houses
on her block. Then she crosses the street

to her neighbor's yellow door, peers
through the mail slot. It's dark in there,

and all she sees is a stack
of blue plates on a table. Where

are the secret drawers filled with cigarettes
and diaries? Where are the boxes of pliers

and hammers, the screws flexing
their tiny shoulders? The needles and gum?

When a spider drifts up toward the ceiling,
the afternoon stops moving. Ella stares

for a long time. Then she blinks,
and the leaves go back to sizzling.

First published in *THE SOUTHERN REVIEW*

POLYPHONIC AUTOPSY OF A WOMAN
WHO MAY NOT andor CANNOT EXIST

the chart below shows the decline in the fire death rate (2006-2015)
before   she

       burned
           they   gouged   out   eyes

                            eyes

                               I's [sic]
                    her

the chart below shows the trend (2006-2015)
[He]

    is

       asking

          me

            about

               Joey [sic]

                  what

                     do

                       I

                         say???

          I saw you in the Daily Beast etc. a little late, no smoke:
the webpage was chalk-white suitable for reading (excess of 700°C)
the text a clear dark brown-black (300°C–400°C)
my head was sent into an ash-like gray (500°C–600°C)
careening against this brown-yellow yellow yellow [sic] (200°C)

FRAGMENTATION OF BURNT BONES & SURVIVAL OF TRAUMA MADE ON BONES

My heart breaking in two, Please help me.
I miss you Joey [sic] dad loves you,
May u rip in peace.
She was scared. Because of ... just scared.

It was an accident. So many trans women these days live in multiple
Ziploc bags. Sleep there. God I am so lucky.
We shared a name once. I have a cousin with two older sisters. Her name/
your name would have been mine if I'd been born a girl [sic] like her.

Keywords: burnt remains, burnt bone, cremation, DNA degradation,
micro-CT
Keywords: when, she, didn't, drink, poison, they, stabbed, her, multiple,
times, in, her, genitals

The other night I was walking home and I got viciously scared.
I wore knee-highs and a knife-
pleated skirt.
I was alone. Every pedestrian was a knife [sic]
or a martini glass of antifreeze, sweet, or gasoline.
That's when I think of you
and you and you and you.

THEM: *the skull almost always stays, for the most part, intact,*
        leaving the brain in relatively good shape [sic]
YOU: *I am beautiful I don't care what people think*
ALSO THEM: *You were supposed to stick to the story*

I checked your social media, the only place you were
out. It was like a ghost town but
with better hair! This past fall mine was
the same color. Sunset. I think we might be the same person
or friends. Let's get engaged [sic]!
I cannot bear the thought of living in a world
without you.

the pie chart below shows causes of outside fires (2015)

other (4.4%)

    act of nature (4.7%)

        under investigation (4.8%)

            intentional (17.1%)   unintentional, careless [sic] (43.1%)

                undetermined (25.9%)

the pie chart below shows (2015)

I

    am

        single   *ugly [sic]*

            probable   *am*

                will   *I*

                        be

I imagine coroners
and forensic scientists
in their Tyvek paper suits.
I imagine ampules of
dark amber, liquid time.
In the corner is a centrifuge
spinning biological tempest.
I want to be
better than them [sic].
I don't think I am.

[instagram user] @[instagram user] *murder*
[instagram user] @[instagram user] *Rest [sic] in power*

All this to say—
dear Not Joey—
this is Joey.
Today   I   found   out
when   bones   burn at 1,100°C they   lose half
their   volume   /weight.   Our world   is like   that   now,
feels   as   insubstantial   as   a   crepe   dove
unfolding   its   lissome   wings
int o   the   Mid west   s ky   [si c].

First published in *BLACK WARRIOR REVIEW*

MORNING IN WEST VIRGINIA

~After Victoria Kelly

I can imagine living a whole life
in my hometown, in Illinois—
on the dock with my father,
peeling back the layers of our secrets,
until what last remains of orange light
burns between the boughs of pines,
and the dark sky spills out of the clouds,
and we head inside to the wood stove—
this place, where, at sixteen, in a used Ford,
I jumped the hills on my way to school,
where, at twenty-one, I fired a bullet
through a gallon of milk, and my father said,
"That's what it does to someone's heart."

I can imagine how different I'd be
if I stayed behind to start each day,
barefoot in the morning light,
shuffling over hardwood,
in my father's footsteps,
from the bed to the coffee pot,
in a home that could've been mine,
had I chosen this life that never happened.

And to think that now,
if I'd chosen differently,

that life could've carried me,
from this lonely, gray morning
in a basement apartment in West Virginia
under the coal-fire sky of autumn—
with Subarus puttering up mountain passes,
and tired students hunched beneath book bags,
walking through a doorway, as if
into a dream that hasn't yet materialized.
Meanwhile under the streetlights on the bridge,
a man, who could be my father, walks away from me,
with a boy, who is sleeping, slung on his back.

First published in *THE FOURTH RIVER*

WHEN WE SING OF MIGHT

i.

In this part I switch clothes with a woman I just met
shed my phone, my metal—pray to the scanner gods.
I walk freely through each lock, each clanging door;
here the prison air, the elastic waist of her patterned skirt
settle like a new identity around my body.

ii.

This is the part where it used to be game—a child
moving like a worm through the blades of cool,
through soft evening grass. Firecrackers our only sin.

From here I watch the patrol car, count to ten to twenty,
count the pointed edges of a star driving by,
remember the chorus about sin and error pining—
hold my breath, spend an old longing born of beer,
born of bible talk and men.

iii.

This is the year when no one followed the tin star
or the wonder star of Christmas hymns,
when the trail between the courthouse and my grandma's
grew shorter and everybody's hands got tired
picking the rice clean enough for baby Jesus,

clean enough to sell at the Model Meat Market
on Main Street where all the cars parked on an angle,
and I used to think the sign said "angel parking"
and I wondered who would park an angel
if they could find one.

iv.

Right here *weary world* I park the flashbacks
about all the arrestable moments—a past of illegal
brown bodies eating out of season, boys the wrong color
for love, a past of too many: fish, fists, and bottles
broken, the brown drip of spilled brandy—arrestable
edges of lives made jagged and dangerous
(*His law is love and His gospel is peace*)
star-jagged and dangerous as the moments where I see
and maybe you do too the faces sharpened
into angles of rage, of disgust sharpened
on all the low-wage jobs and lying songs
their children learned in grade school
and sang at concerts with fingerplay
and warm kool-aid, when we all still drank
the kool-aid and believed the liberty lyrics—
(*and in His name all oppression shall cease*).

This is the part where arrestable moments
could go either way—and do

depending upon the time of night
the county and the star-wearing body.
So that quiet grass and breath-holding
was training. That counting, one to ten,
ten to twenty—this is where
seconds can become years for some
when it goes the wrong way
when they are the wrong color
when their pockets are empty
when liberty and justice for all—is all used up.

v.

But when we sing of might, this is the part
the part where my jailed brown uncles
my shackled cousins angel their way in
where children fostered and lost reappear.
I dress in their stories patterned and purple
as night. I dress in old songs of prison trains
and men covering their eyes to sleep,
songs of women on one side of a sliding panel
of lives shattered but mosaiced by might—
the angles of survival a many-cornered wholeness.

First published in *LITERARY HUB*

OH WONDER

It's the garden spider who eats her mistakes
at the end of day so she can billow in the lung
of night, dangling from an insecure branch

or caught on the coral spur of a dove's foot
and sleep, her spinnerets trailing radials like
ungathered hair. It's a million pound cumulus.

It's the stratosphere, holding it, miraculous. It's
a mammatus rolling her weight through dusk
waiting to unhook and shake free the hail.

Sometimes it's so ordinary it escapes your notice—
pothos reaching for windows, ease of an avocado
slipping its skin. A porcelain boy with lamp-black

eyes told me most mammals have the same average
number of heartbeats in a lifetime. It is the mouse
engine that hums too hot to last. It is the blue whale's

slow electricity—six pumps per minute is the way
to live centuries. I think it's also the hummingbird
I saw in a video lifted off a cement floor by firefighters

and fed sugar water until she was again a tempest.
It wasn't when my mother lay on the garage floor
and my brother lifted her while I tried to shout louder

than her sobs. But it was her heart, a washable ink.
It was her dark's genius, how it moaned slow enough
to outlive her. It is the orca who pushes her dead calf

a thousand miles before she drops it or it falls apart.
And it is also when she plays with her pod the day
after. It is the night my son tugs at his pajama

collar and cries: The sad is so big I can't get it all out,
and I behold him, astonished, his sadness as clean
and abundant as spring. His thunder-heart, a marvel

I refuse to invade with empathy. And outside, clouds
groan like gods, a garden spider consumes her home.
It's knowing she can weave it tomorrow between

citrus leaves and earth. It's her chamberless heart
cleaving the length of her body. It is lifting my son
into my lap to witness the birth of his grieving.

First published in *32 POEMS*

GOING DEAF

For a while it's mostly bliss,
swimming a lovely, negotiable
lake, the hush of small fish,

or like resting inside a shell,
a turtle, a nutmeat, a swaddled
babe, pacified and riding

the sweet blurry line between
stillness and sleep. But later
you wonder whether the lake

is a roiling ocean you are
alone in with sharks, other
predators, and water pressure

or a kind of padded cell, you
the slow prisoner who wonders
if anyone else will show up

to bring you poetry or mass or
whatever you yearn for—a bible,
cigarettes, kisses, a knife in a cake.

First published in *FLYING ISLAND*

———

COUNTY 19

I twist in my seat beside the woman who picked me up
on County 19, reaching back to help her son
eat his Happy Meal. I fly a french fry through the air,
thinking how weird it is to hitch a ride on the road
I've driven so many times with my dad—
the route between our house and the old folks home
where Grandma lasted alone for fourteen years.
Each time we visited: the veins wider, bluer,
the ankles thinner, the distances between bedsores
diminished, the cheer my dad convinced himself to feel
as he repeated the litany: I am your son.
This is your grandson. We're so happy to see you.
The woman asks me where I'm going
and I say as far as you can take me,
but as we pass the old folks home I tell her to pull over.
The boy is finished with his Happy Meal and now
he points at the bruise on his elbow and says Ouch.
His mom nods at him in the rearview as I get out.
That's right, she says. Ouch. There is the low roofline,
the sign with a bible quote in changeable letters,
my grandma's old window as blank as it was
when she lived here, some earth dug up
in the bordering cornfield for construction
of a new wing. I think about barging through the doors
and demanding to see Elizabeth Wee, making
some kind of scene. I think about setting up camp
in the hole in the cornfield and refusing to leave.

But instead I wander the grounds for awhile.
I lie in the parking lot's grass island and watch
the cornstalks feather the road with lank shadows,
the sunlight dipping down into the tassels.
I want speed. I want new people. To ditch
this slow sanitary drain of golden light,
my pastor parents and their immovable faith,
this town's brown river exhausting its banks.
Elizabeth is underground. So is my cousin.
Markers like polished teeth in the family plot.
In the twilight I walk back to the shoulder
and catch a ride from a farmer hauling a trailer
stacked with hay bales three-high. When he asks me
where I'm going I say as far as you can take me.

First published in *THE LOW PASSIONS*

SIX REASONS I CAN'T ANSWER THE DOOR FOR HIM
AT 3 IN THE MORNING

The last man here wanted what cannot be taken:
my girl, he'd say, my baby.

The narrow of his eyes
scattered mice in the walls.

A man before him hid cans in high cabinets.
Neighbors slipped notes through the breezeway:

Just yell help, they said.
Police respond quick here—

Here as in not someplace else.

Then there's Brother who can't come home at Christmas.

The girl he says he don't know
in my same sweatshirt
when they pulled her from the creek.

In the city where we were born,
bullets crawl blocks like brush fire,
spent casings end up in water.

Police come to the door,
ask for men we can't name.

Now—tucked between my hip bone
and my ribcage—
I'm growing another body.

The lady who does the ultrasounds
says she'll be a girl like me.

If we believe what God says about Adam:
his rib bone and his finger-pointing,
we know it falls to other girls to pass the warning:

There are men who sleep
and men who don't,
and it's up to us to know the difference.

It falls to me to teach her
a door is also a thing that opens—
even a deadbolt is still a kind of hope.

First published in *RATTLE*

ROBIN CHAPMAN

THE POET'S HOUSE

i.m. Susan Elbe (1946-2017)

Scrim of black and white
in fireplace grate and mantel,
rug and chair, obelisk
and inuksuk, raven
and black bear--

her winter house
evoked the early dark,
micaceous clay, flare
of light on warping ice,
chink and glitz of it
in moon-glow milk,

flint words struck to make
the spark reflected
in the wolf's dark pupil,
his ruff of fur,
a lantern lifted
against the night.

First published in *NORTH AMERICAN REVIEW*

HOMETOWN NOCTURNE

When I can't sleep, I remember it: blue fields
of night I'd slip into, my borrowed coat
and secondhand boots trailing frayed laces
through curbside sleet and neighbors' lawns,
the poplars lanky and indifferent as teenagers,
the moon a spitball on the back of heaven's
dark shirt. Some nights a boy would wait
in a car humming down the street, thumbs
drumming the wheel and the tailpipe panting.
But more often the ones I liked didn't drive, got all A's
and ran cross-country, had parents that kept them
from me, tongued my name like a secret
sweet. A good Muslim girl, I kissed mostly
above the belt, prayed when I had to, and when I slid
lipstick into my sleeve at the drugstore I felt bad about it,
I was very good at feeling bad. The sky fell regularly
in little white stars that caught in my hair. The air
singed my lungs, exhaled as tinsel. I shadowed
streets heading nowhere, asphalt erased
beneath a fresh sheet, season of rimed windows
and bated breath by the radio. In every living room,
some kind of nocturnal glow—plastic menorahs'
tongues of flame, cheap bulbs burning in fir branches,
a night-light shaped like a man of snow or God.
And in darker rooms our parents fell asleep
on their backs watching reruns, our brothers

clicked on videos of squirming blondes in the trembling
glare of computer screens, while somewhere else,
in a bar or basement, prized Midwestern jewels gleamed
in the bellies of college girls, Burnett's
swirling in a cup, and the tiny planets
of ping-pong balls circling Solo rims.
Like this, I orbited the town of my origin,
slogged familiar paths of salt-marbled sidewalks,
ringed cul-de-sacs and parking lots and potholes'
gritty ice rinks. The hooded eyes of houses
looked on and past me. The huddled trees
whispered, brandished pom-poms just for show.
I carved carefully my name in frost.
Scuffed my feet the whole way home.

First published in *NARRATIVE*

___

MOVEMENT:

I don't know what will happen, but I'd like to have a say. The most terrible feelings are followed by euphoria. A sensation of a tiny me swimming in stomach. Then: land. The relief when endorphins release. My therapist tells me that in times of fear I can remember three joyful moments in my life and be grateful. She says sheepishly that she heard this idea from Oprah. I, half listening to what she says next, try to find these moments but what are they? Memory is difficult now. People say remember Mom and Dad, the good times. I recall my mother's face smiling between each railing as I began walking down the stairs, but I don't. I remember the fast food breakfasts my father brought home Saturday mornings after he taught yoga. We ate upstairs with Mom, newspaper tablecloth on the bed. How do I feel about my childhood? This is a question I do not ask. Rather, how has their murder affected me? Innumerable. You want me to qualify, but I choose to quantify. I live between bookends of innumerable. I run between both ends, stop, plead for rest, get lost in forests, stay for some time alone, but run again because society thinks it strange, thinks I am strange, been called broken, but I refuse that title. That language.

First published in *THE MASSACHUSETTS REVIEW*

ROAD TRIP

after "Road Trip" by Gary Carlson

Some groups of birds are called
a different name depending upon
which element they're in: A flock

of ducks in the sky or a paddling
of ducks on the water, for example.
Has someone forgotten to question

a traditional structure? We were,
as convention dictates, called a family
when we were near one another and

also when we were farther.
Topography
noticed occasionally

as a nice backdrop to our
ancestral spectacle-on-wheels
as we sought more suitable

terrain for what's unnamable
in each one of us. Nobody
related to this scene

has ever called any collection
of any birds a paddling.
Even on vacation, we called

what we were making progress:
that old saw, camper in tow. For no
other reason than to cast

our personal shadows across
plural national monuments?
Shed antler discovered at a meadow's

threshold: Can we keep it? Or any
small token of a world
we don't belong to? Why don't we?

This whole voyage is beginning
to sound autobiographical, but it's
inspired by a profound nostalgia

for nostalgia. Back inside
the bell jar of the imagination, I mean
the station wagon, moods

domino, a Rube-Goldberg
contraption. We didn't know
why we were fighting. So close

for so long. Then we weren't.
Then we were again
passing a road sign

that read: PRISON
AREA DO NOT PICK
UP HITCHHIKERS.

Inside the high fence we
travel by and soon forget, lives
a group of humans often called

by different names than human.
Anybody related to this scene might
have family lost in there.

See the landscape roll by, that parched
red of memory's false heat. See the birds,
whatever they're called, borrowing the sky.

First published in *EKPHRASIS*

_____

IF WE HAD A LEMON WE'D THROW IT AND CALL THAT THE SUN

and that was one thing quickly becoming another
~Gerald Stern, *"Red Wool Bathrobe"*

I'd like to invite you to the party but I don't
know your name, have your address, or
know you well enough to really want you
around my cat. I feel a kinship with all people
and then I share a beach with them and want
to yell use your inside voice. We're outside
but that doesn't mean we'll not dissolve
if raised to the light. Some days the sea wants
to chew us into shattered two-by-fours.
Some days she's a kitten pasting soft hairs
around our ankles. I know—I know this for
a fact—there are moist pasta salads being
prepared and eaten all around me—in those
bushes for instance—and I'm not getting any.
I tried to start my life out right and still
lost track of where I was going. Example,
I picked my college because my girlfriend
went there. She slept with my best friend.
I went there anyway. That determined
the course of the rest of my life. I wiped
the table down with bleach before sitting
and now my forearm smells. It's going
to be okay though. I'm going to need this
bleach-arm for some purpose. To identify

some wanderers in the sky it's helpful to
determine the color. At a distance everything
for me goes gray. A mountain range in
a black-and-white film. We've been walking,
my horse and I, for days. For water we
think about rivers and lick our own ideas.

First published in *GULF COAST*

GEORGE DAVID CLARK

───

ULTRASOUND: YOUR PICTURE

—Henry Thomas Clark, 10/7/14

We've framed an ultrasound
    of you and Peter

holding hands
    (or almost) in the womb,

your moon-bright arms
    crossed in a black balloon

with week, and weights,
    and heights in millimeters

penciled on the side.
    We say it's good

that he, at least, was with you
    when you died,

that unlike us
    you'll never know the why

of being lonely
    or what naked falsehood

feels like in one's mind.
    You see, it's false

to say your death
        was somehow grace. It's grace

that spared Cain's life
        and later gave Eve other

sons, despite creation's
        wastes and faults.

I wish you could have known
        love's aftertastes.

I wish you'd had a chance
        to hate your brother.

First published in *THE HOPKINS REVIEW*

TIANA CLARK

VIRTUE SIGNALING, WISCONSIN

You couldn't know this loneliness... –Natalie Eilbert

My first night in Madison   the air was different—
cool, less sticky. The street   was quiet, weirdly   stagnant.
Our house, a pale yellow.   I straddled the   isthmus,
felt ice chip   between both lakes   like frozen lace.
I'm hyper   visible now,   so seen, so   everywhere, then suddenly
nowhere—so much so, I became   Muzak   to my own face.
Now   I'm being   followed   inside a grocery store. Down each aisle,
then back again. Now I'm being   stalked   inside a restaurant.
I switch seats.   But it does not matter.   I feel it all: the eyeballs
of this town scorch   the back of my neck,   skin already darker there.
I want to pluck   all the signs   I see stapled across
these manicured lawns   that read: Black Lives Matter.
I don't believe you.   There is a sign you buy because
you want so badly to believe   in what it has to say,
and then there is a sign you buy   because
                you want others to believe you are brave.
A sign can't save   my life?   You will not spare me.
I watch   as you watch me   I watch
as my white students watch me   I watch me   watch me, smaller now
than when I first moved here.   Lost a quarter of an inch
my doctor said.   Most days   I wait
for the bitter winter to end.   Most days   I wait   for another black
person to pass me.   Most days   they never come.
Most days I wait   for another black person   to save me
and we hold the gaze.   We do not smile or lie.   A simple nod
simply   saves my life.

First published in *THE LOS ANGELES REVIEW*

CARRIED

When I'm sick, I wish whatever song is in my head
would stop. Tonight, it's the same tune my mother sang
to tuck me in, its notes the kind of kindness
only distant trains still hit—soft like a string
of Christmas lights sort-of smiling from a darkened
window—the same tune I took up,
humming some, to steel myself against the fruit-like
odor shrouding my boy's room—his sick bed, stuffed bear
and the bucket beside him— too dull to be sweet,
too thick to breathe. Some days, the house seems crowded
with intruders— on the stairs, the countertops,
and windowpane, all murmuring a prelude to descent—
the days I walk bags full of liquid to the curb, still bodywarm,
so that the drips turn steam before they hit
the filthy snow. Yet, when he reached to take my hands—
then cracked from nervous washing—there was nothing
more I wanted than to hold him, and that old song
was enough to soothe us, huddled there and praying
that the angel would depart. Tonight, there's no one here
except me, and that song is stuck, rattling through
my enfeebled frame like a fly caught in a screen, or
some stray moisture in a lung. Sometimes, when the melody
dies down, a well-forgotten dream or memory persists
to take its place, the outline of a church pew's
scuffed wood, enduring my mother's nervous fingernails
and a child's thoughtless graffiti—blue marker that won't
wash off, years after—while the preacher asks

o death, where is thy sting? I used to think
the price of dying was detachment, a severing
from what we gather of the world—these flimsy
souvenirs—our songs, the memories we don't want,
and the ones we do, the long nights by my son's bed
almost whispering you are my sunshine, while the wind
rails inexplicably against the window. I wonder
if I get too sick, how will I know? And who will take me
to the hospital, orphaned as I am—as everybody
comes to be, with time—if the fever renders me
incapable of calling? I don't know what my mother saw
before she went to sleep the last time, but
when I get sick— and pray so hard for silence
that I think I might become it—I hear my boy
begin to sing, and then, become the song.

First published in *PLOUGHSHARES*

J. L. CONRAD

MIRACLE TOWN

in which everything is cast aside

We choose, for instance, to take off our skins. Our bones sheltering the soft animals of our organs. In the white light of a winter moon, we parade together, bandying about. Some carry flags. Others have stitched small triangles of cloth together to form a banner. A word that comes to mind is *festoon*. Another is *shimmy*. We make our way out not knowing the way back. Together the bones of our feet chatter. The city a long knife lying between two blue eyes. The city a bridge we take toward an after in which we will have learned, as it turns out, nothing. Wind blows itself out against our foreheads. Flags flap on their slender poles. The moon like a coin on the lid of each closed eye.

First published in *SALT HILL*

CAITLIN COWAN

WHAT STILLNESS IS

for Trista

"Faintings 110; shrieks 20 (per performance); left theater
(first act 19); left theater (second act 150), left theater (third
act 1); returned (after revival) 100; returned visit 10 (per
performance); husbands summoned to escort home wives 10
(per performance); taxicab increase 500%"
— *Dracula*'s First Seven Weeks at the Biltmore Theater,
LA TIMES, AUGUST 1928

In the theater the women faint   we've been at it for years
our collapsing   & quaking our crumpling   at blood & bile
But I've done one better: I faint & they gild   my pockets
I know what stillness is   my sisters too   this our sole inheritance
this our heart's white desert   You know the scene: woman alone
in the kitchen woman   alone at her needlework woman
alone   eyes rolled to snowdrift—heart slowing   slowed
I will be your nothing; I already am   Your empty
post-show glow your canary   in a coffin: its only song
the quiet   of an angry husband's house I am   the greatest fainting
woman in the world   this is no act You see   we slip out of time:
our tiny black escapes   & then back in: we bleed to life
before the Count's empty reflection   He is not there; that is
his terror & ours   now Lugosi feasts on Lucy   his endless
thirst unslaked until   a man unsheathes his favorite weapon
impaling the creature   he stuffs the shiv inside him deep
The whalebone sucks   our skinny ribs   squeezes my sisters
to exhaustion   but I am full   of breath & power—   my faint

is no fear   I got paid while they burned him & his film

turned to smoke like my sisters long ago   Do not fear the stillness—

the closed casket &   the monster it births   Fear what's born

from the quiet   womb before the storm   This is my house &

I'm on the floor   my pain sells tickets puts asses in seats

When you turn out the lights   remember every evil   is born

of woman   I don't have to kill you; you're   already dead

Without us is no us   so bring the smelling salts Watch me

drink the darkness   honey   I've got bills to pay

First published in *BAD PONY*

_____

NO TONGUE CAN TELL

You start by saying you'd rather live anywhere
else, and jump from the weather to roadwork to how
the lack of gay bars in this town makes you itch. You swear
you saw a guy at Wal-Mart slick his hair

with Vaseline. I never did that, but I know
boys who did: jocks with camo caps and torn leather
boots. I'm still crammed in the same state with different kinds
of clueless guys. I look at you, and you raise

another shot in salute. I'm gin-lipped and racing
my fingers through my bale of hair. It's easy
for a boy who's spent his life at the edge of orchards
to believe in rebirth. Everyone from the Midwest stocks

curses in their cheeks. We serve our spite
on plates of cheese. We sing Bob Dylan
to our cattle. Listen, I could be your boy. I could be unshaved
arms, the voice to break each morning like a lamp.

Just tell me you want to stay, to see
how every storm blots a rainbow over the beach.
I want your fists in a sand dune. I want you
to lick the gristle caught between my teeth. Trust me,
I know what it's like to have the smallest parade.

First published in *SPLIT ROCK REVIEW*

ALEXANDRIA DELCOURT

―――

THE MARCOS HIGHWAY

For Christmas the stars have descended
from the perches of night to hang
like dusty dreams from the ceiling,
streamers of yellow and blue dangling
below in the humid breeze next to
dried meat, candy, bananas. The war
never ended here, merely hid itself
in the violent heat, disguised the sky
as a tangle of black wire, crept up
onto the sides of buildings like ghostly
handprints. In the middle of it all, you
sit beneath a cracked Coca-Cola sign
by the road's side like a strange
postcard I might have picked up
somewhere. I take a picture
of the sign, your ripped cargo shorts,
and in it you look contemplative.
I assume you are thinking of family,
how far away you are for the holiday.
I don't ask. The rest of us
crowd into the van like chickens,
breathing sweat, trying to swim
the space between America and here
as if thousands of miles could fit
into a single human skull without
the stretching involved in atomic
expansion - enough to pull the heavens

down, to twist time into a rope,
a rope into a noose. Outside the
tinted windows, the deep jungle
falls away into valleys as
we rise like believers above the clouds,
arrive beneath unexpected pine,
magnolias, everything upside down,
we and you somehow surviving.

First published in *POWER: PUBLIC POETRY ANTHOLOGY*

DARREN C. DEMAREE

———

[you might choose to read these poems]

i told my children you might choose to read these poems in the bareness
and anxiety of your young adulthood while you search for me in the
thousands and thousands of poems i've written so that i could explore
so that i could explain so that i could hide and lie about some small
terribleness and it gives me endless joy that you will find me here right
here right now as bare as you are but feeling no anxiety at all because
i am with my children in some small way in the future when i love you
even more than i already do because that's how real love works it grows
with the epic it encircles the epic until you cannot tell why or how any of
this began but you know you know you know that if there is such a thing
as a soul it exists to be buoyed by moments like this

First published in *WHALE ROAD REVIEW*

HEATHER DERR-SMITH

—

AMERICAN READY CUT SYSTEM HOUSES

Your postcard said, *Nothing like a little disaster to sort things out.*

Blueprints, sketches, such perfect houses in the photograph on the front,
all the lines true and in harmony. I took it with me like a paper charm,

searching for home, hit the road, looking for the exact spot
of my birthright, down the rustling path of thistles and nettles,

under a leaden sky, in the place where God once lifted

the home by its hair, nothing left but the kitchen and the
bathtub where we all hid. The supper table

picked up and carried to the county over and laid so gently down.

When I saw you last in the bar in Brooklyn, you told me to sing.
But I couldn't even speak. I laid my head in your lap,

drunk at two am and felt your hand resting across my back,
reluctant, unsure of what I wanted, but knowing

it was a want too much for anyone to give in to, a halter
broke, some rip.

The skeletons of the trees are coming back to life now, sap like stars
risen again. Most anything torn can be mended. No real

permanent damage. The land where the house was
goes back to the plum-colored dusk, hooks and hoods of the hawks

perching in the Hemlocks, clouds and mounds of nebulae in the sky in
the pitch night.

Frank Lloyd Wright said, *nature will never fail you*, though, I suppose it
depends

on what you mean by *fail*. It'll kill you for sure, Great Revelator.

You can hear the wilderness ad-libbing its prayers in the whip-poor-will
and the cypress,

in the percussion and boom of bittern in the bulrushes.

Dead is the mandible, alive the song, wrote Nabokov.

The bones of our houses, the house of our bones
dropped in a sudden blur of wind and wings,

but our voices still throb and palpitate somewhere, by some rapture,
in memory's ear, in the fluttering pages, behind the stars.

I have a song now I want to sing to you, but you're long gone.
When you said I'm here for you, was that a promise?

Overwhelm,

to bury or drown beneath a huge mass

Whelmen: *to turn upside down*

To turn over and over like a boat washed over and overset by a wave

To bring to ruin.

The end of one part of the world, a story that no longer has a witness.

But I'll sing it to myself. I'll sing it to the small moth,
the size of scarcely a word,

Ad libitum, according to my desire.

First published in THRUST

SEPTIMANIA

—*After Adam Hochschild's Spain in Our Hearts*

When I check to see which exit I should use
when emerging from the Lesseps Metro stop,
the map says *Septimania*, and instead of thinking
of that ancient borderland that once existed
between France and Spain, I remember
the septic tank at the center of my childhood
backyard, the contents of which were so full
of our excrement that our grass glowed
emerald green for decades until the town managers
decided to create whole rivers of putrefaction
streaming underneath the road into sewage systems
that would have made ancient Romans proud.
I take Septimania, emerge from the bowels
of the earth, walk 290 meters, and arrive
at the door of my son's preschool, where he
has been baking bread for the past hour.
There's something so precious about the lightness
of that activity, all that leavening and rising,
that I laugh when the headmaster tells me
about three-year-olds baking bread every day.
He looks at me and says, *Why are you laughing?*
The bread is delicious! Yes, headmaster,
yes to lightness and rising, even if
I needed to wade through putrefaction
to get to it. On an ordinary day, rottenness

is trending, but in the days since the inauguration,
excrement has become all the rage—one day
of news from America is enough to convince
anyone of that. It seems, though, that war
has always been a magnet for fundament.
Just today, I was re-reading George Orwell's
Homage to Catalonia, and I marveled
at his attention to diarrhea, decaying food,
and the horse dung of the Spanish Civil War.
Later, I learned from Adam Hochschild
that the women who belonged to unions
and yearned for a classless society
were objects of such enmity that everything
needed to be taken from them. Sometimes
the soldiers took their newborns; sometimes
Franco's soldiers tattooed the women's flesh
with the yoke and arrows of the Falangists;
sometimes the soldiers gang-raped the women
and then bragged about it to anyone
who would listen; sometimes, if the women
still resisted the power of tyranny, they
were forced to drink castor oil, a powerful
laxative, and then parade through the streets,
being jeered as they soiled themselves. Today
is another beautiful day, radiant with Mediterranean
sun, even in January. My son and I walk
to Plaça del Diamant, the site of the old

air-raid shelter, and a bronze statue of a woman
whose naked body seems to rise and break
through the earth. At first, her pose suggests
that she is an emblem of freedom, but no.
Her stance is one of both terror and amazement.
The bronze eviscerates her body, breaking it
in two. In the plaza, we do what all
the other families do: play "crazy car"
with his balance bike, buy candy at the Supermercat,
then descend again into the underworld
of the Metro, as if everyone knows
what happened here, and who belonged to whom.

First published in *NEW ENGLAND REVIEW*

NICOLE M. K. EIDEN

_____

MORTGAGE

This house that we built is lovely
Here, I sleep next to you every night

Remember when we were unfamiliar. I had a plump life
you had a plump life

we were busy with our things
we tried to be loved by other people

Remember that messy life

_____

But then, as they say, we got together
we had sex everyday

Who knew when I would ask the wrong question
The instant you would turn dull

But you weren't scared of scrambled eggs
You were keen to walk the dog

And now here we are every night

_____

It's after midnight, sapped from balancing plates, people all night for cash
Exhausted from nailing floorboards and keeping hair off the tub

My calves ache and I don't want to give
It's the end of the month is there enough for the mortgage

I want to buy a hardback atlas, the book that split
the Germanys, took me to the USSR

pressed my kindergarten watercolors   proved
my humble town existed

The atlas is $80
But we need toothpaste

I want to see a movie – can't, can't, there's not enough
it's the end of the month

I move away from you. Find your own dinner.
Do you want something or are you just hugging me good night?

––––––––––––

The 1st comes – we pay the mortgage, another month
You reach out again. Your hand says Come here

All weighty words fall second to the comfort we create
I don't wonder what you want. I quickly kiss you hard.

First published in *I AM ONE OF YOU*

IN THE NUNNERY OF WATER

I was born there, between water
and sand. The water was clear
exactly once. Then, I could see
all things playing out just right,
like a memory germinating
into my inner earth; only
movement could change
the outcome. Movement
muddied the future. The creek
is not perfect, but it was home
despite the snakes and leeches
and movement. I was a mermaid
in a Midwestern creek so clear
it was a religion; my vows
were a song that sounded
so much like the wind kissing
oak leaves and the clearest water;
like tree roots baptizing a mermaid
who had no business being
anywhere else but in the wet;
like rocks softening to the touch
of a creek's harsh love and a mermaid's
last song. I did not sing a love song
when all I know are elegies about water
and movement and a future I will never
see coming. I guess I never stood a chance.

First published in *RAW ART REVIEW*

BENT

My stepbrother and I played hide-and-seek naked after our parents
had gone to sleep. Our skin drank air as we ran room-
to-room, transparent daffodils. Freedom in bareness,
in the folds of our undeveloped bodies uninhibited, blooming

stamen. Once they woke up to find us nude on the floor,
six-year-olds examining each other in inquiry. My mother's
still-drunk-slurs, *Disgraceful*, like aphid secretions forming
mildew on our petals. The next day they smothered

our roots and pruned us. *Two boys can't be naked together.*
Are you gay? A few years later I would tell mom I might
be while driving from Indianapolis to Chicago. Ether-
words burning her ears, though she didn't put up a fight.

When I was sixteen, mom passed out drunk, naked on the floor,
I carried her to bed that night, keeping quiet when I shut the door.

First published in *THE MATADOR REVIEW*

_____

DAILY NEWS

Oh bodies, where are you?
I hear the flowers, the pines,
the lizards mourn even in their silence.

We are silent too, even when we
ask where are the bodies, where are
the bodies in ash in sky, where

can we find comfort, and how?
The leaves shake in shadow on the shades
and you cannot leave the house, you cannot

leave the neighborhood, you cannot find
the bodies, the bodies, where are the bodies?
They say there are children there, being burned

alive [they say the old woman pushes them
in the oven and burns them alive, they say]
the armies are closing in and

all it takes is a match, the armies are closing in
and [the mothers, the mothers, it's always
the mothers] [there is nothing left

for them to bury.] Bluebeard lifts his
hatchet every time he comes back
home from war. Scheherazade
fashions a new story every time

her boss comes to her. We listen
to the stories, ask where are the bodies
where are the bodies? Everyone

knows that today, children were burned
alive. The television screens are fired
up behind the shades. Eyelids fall

because who tells the tales? Who listens?
Who lights the match and watches
the children burn? Today, children burn.

First published in *JET FUEL REVIEW*

MOLLY FULLER

THE TALE OF THE FLOPSY BUNNIES

All the girls in the yellow wing of the hospital give birth to rabbits at
the same time in the same day. The nurses bundle them up in pink and
blue. The new mothers coo and rub their soft, velvet heads. They call
them by the names they have rehearsed for sons and daughters. The
fathers smoke cigars and drink whiskey. The grandmothers weep and
knit bonnets with holes for small ears. The grandfathers watch from their
rockers, peeling carrots for stew.

First published in _ALL NATIONS PRESS_

MAX GARLAND

———

BAT IN THE HOUSE

What you hear in sleep is the swim of live leather
as the bat sweeps over your face on the pillow,
takes his laps around the room,
at each turn unravels
a little more than you dreamed
until the last thread is fear
and there you are.

Consider the naked skin, how much it takes
to reach the lamp, eyeglasses, the last shirt
thrown down.

Consider a bracelet of bat, a livid tattoo.
Consider the strangeness
of sixty squeaks per second
bouncing back from your body.

You've gone into this before.
You've read how clean they are,
how well they hear the shape of a thing,
how little harm they mean.

You've tried to outfox fear with learning,
but the chemical self is newborn each night.
The bedtime heart is the world's worst student.

Later, when you've managed it, wielded
the fish net and broom, heard the screechings

of the tangled creature, counted the bared,
tiny beautiful teeth
and coaxed the bat to freedom,
you feel humane, but unconsoled.

Every wink of the curtain, every wind has life.
Chiroptera is the name of the order, flying hand.
And the night seems one thick flock,
between the blotted moon and where

you lie and close your eyes
and try not to know, but know
your brother, flying blind—

squinch-face, baby-tooth--
much easier to save than love,
will come again in sleep.

First published in *THE GETTYSBURG REVIEW*

———

APPENDIX

the beginning of a line at the top of the page, the end of a kind of rhythm
we needed to waltz, the you are for me & I am for you, the knees shaking,
the I love you's, the softness, the tulip, thighs, the alliteration repeating,
the heads full of dreams, the empty pools, your cousin Martina grinding
money into the puddle of a hotel sink, singing a kind of song, eyes
twitching, you standing over by the window, your piece of the cut, your
hero taking up with the heroine, my bok choy, my smokeless taboo,
crescent moon, armpit on the nightstand, swollen lymph nodes, my
Robert Mapplethorpe poem, your cousin in jail, wearing our disguises,
you as a housekeeper, me becoming everything I never wanted, the
conversations overheard one table over, the code-switching, *su intenso
dolor abdominal*, the dolphins pink in the river, a hyena, the pet fee &
three children we couldn't afford, maybe God, maybe the dead, maybe
the trespasses against us talking weather & recipes, the anatomy of clams,
the decoy of a pond calling out to its wooden duck, Christmas & summers
in plaster of Paris, your red scarf, triumphant revenge, your look that said
kill, your shot ripping through my motorcade, sending everything into
extinction.

First published in *OVENBIRD POETRY*

———

TIP OF THE TONGUE

That they laid their hands on me I can attest,
The Bible group standing around my chair
As if the Union meeting room we gathered in
Was open tundra and I was fire.
But of the murmuring, the subintelligible
Buzzing like their gift was a plague of wasps
And not the tongue, I say only that I heard
Language I did not recognize, even to know
I did not know it. I wasn't fire. I was the glow
Buried inside the frozen artesian well
I skidded to with friends on the crisp burn
Of the Alfred, NY, midnight while in the sky
A comet quickly becoming a household name
Jettisoned its dead weight.
As its ice melted, the ground ice formed.
A field day for the astromancers.
Sometimes I prayed the comet would crash down
Into the village for the sake of event—
We did not seem to live in interesting times.

I do not know what they were praying for.
The farmer placed the red lamp by the well
Each winter because he knew the ice would come.
But what if, one morning, the sun did not arise?
When the Great Ice retreated from this valley
It left behind the ragged steps of moraines,
Debris to make our chase more difficult.

It won't be long until we beg for ice.
A small, hospital-cupful. Please, sir.
But I digress. I know they were praying.
I believe their intentions were good.

First published in *BIRMINGHAM POETRY REVIEW*

GAIL GRIFFIN

———

DEVASTATED

It's what everybody says they are now.
Your favorite restaurant goes out of business,
you're devastated. Your kid doesn't make
the swim team—devastated. Your one-nighter
fails to call again—you get my drift.
No one hears in the word the cities burning
or sees the ruined fields. It means *laid waste*,
as in *Getting and spending, we lay waste
our powers.* Wordsworth, what's he on about,
I ask my students. Nobody has a clue.
They think he means we throw our powers away
like waste, like Styrofoam, or that we waste them
(whatever they might be, these powers
of ours) like money—not entirely wrong, yet
not right. OK, try Jagger then: *I'll lay
your soul to waste?* Nope, nada. Within
the hour two or three of them will say
they're devastated by their grade or some
abrasive text appearing on their screen.
Words—what can we say about them? Slick,
absorbent, malleable, they mostly fall
apart. And then again, sometimes they hold:
two strange Englishmen, poised at the dawn
and dusk of the industrial West, imagine
the soul as ravaged, leveled landscape, void
of life or color, or of movement, save

the smoke meandering from exhausted fires.
I don't know how to tell you my story,
but if I say that for a certain while
I was devastated, I want you
to smell the fetid smoke, to see the dog,
starving and cankerous, nosing the waste.

First published in *THE SOUTHERN REVIEW*

SUSAN GRIMM

IN FEAR OF BEGINNINGS

Things shift. You see a hearse but it's not for you. No black
dress yet. No tarting up the fatwood log with questionable

paints. That's why I grip the edge of spring so hard, grind
my teeth on the winter salt. Do not go in fear of beginnings.

Makeshift/horseshit/slipshod. Start with two dreams. Bones
a crossroad. Spring like a dirty wish. A girl like a cannonball.

Altitude, fuse. A nice blight dress, a very ice dress. I was a star
about to dissolve. I was a star in the lurk of the parking lot.

First published in *SUGAR HOUSE REVIEW*

BOOK OF ERROR

To see and fail to speak from far
away of seeing, to go about
a life, to write to
friends and of them,
to begin within
their names, to wish them well
and end in yours, sincerely,
to drive to work
in a green car singing,
to have insurance, to listen
to the radio, the county
road in autumn,
the light collected
in the maples, in the birches,
beautiful, to mouth
the words of others,
to believe them,
to feel their language
is your own, to own them
momentarily, to feel ashamed
of owning, to stare
into the open
windows of your house,
to stand beside
your wife, in the center
of your yard, living,
breathing, in the middle

of October, the leaves
around you, everywhere
around you, to watch your daughter,
to listen to her laughter
fill you. From far away
across the yard, it fills you.
And then to know within the poem
the noise that other
people make
when suffering. Enough
to love them, to wish them well, you needed
them imagined. You made
them up, the people.
What are people?
And so it was you came
to speak alone, a soul composed
beyond the finite boundary
of an ethics. Etched
into an opening and closing
space, the sound of "it" compressed with "it is not,"
their echoing, your ache

First published in *Orient*

ROY G. GUZMÁN

———

BLOOD FANTASIA

a loose cento-sestina

I am cosmically outrageous,   a tragic orchestra. Mother dressed him
   in guava-colored lace crinolines   and the silence of the orchid.
His head, a smashed
piñata of bone and blood,   a country with 180,000 orphans, the irony
   of barbed wire.

                         We step over the barbed wire   into the pasture,
outrageous
flowers as big as human / heads.   The truth is you can be orphaned
again
   and again and again.   Where my mother once peddled guavas,
she sat a small Dora piñata in her lap   and read a piece about Freud's
Dora
   case study of hysteria,   putting the two Doras in dialogue with one
another,
concealed among orchids of subtle idiosyncrasy.

                              In the orchid garden, winter
   like a barbed-wire sash on a white gown   for *piñatas* to line
themselves up
in the snow.   The outrageous Pentecostal rush: a flesh-pink guava
   growing inside you.   Pewter seedlings became moonlight   orphans,

orphans are the only ones who get to choose their fathers—   the ghastly
orchid.   I say guava and mean childhood   stuck in a barb wire snare.
Outrageous   when I'm on the scene   so he'd get the first whack
   at the piñata.

     Well, what's in the piñata? they asked.   This orphan,
this foundling, this outcast.   Outrageous   when I'm at a party,
  my hot mouth for an orchid.   No bars, no barbed wire, no pulping
of books—   the guava of independence.

              Pyramids of onion, guava,
melon—all defy.   Flare like a shocked piñata   crisscrossed the sky
   like barbed wire.   The Baudelaire orphans climbed aboard, wide-
mouthed orchids.   Bibliography   is outrageous.

            Poor little orphan boy
of five: The haunches of dead lovers gleam   as clear in skulls   as in
the orchid's velvet crust.   Outrageous / when I
             move   my body—.

       First published in *JET FUEL REVIEW*

Lines taken from:
1.   Vicente Huidobro's *Altazor*.
2.   William H. Dickey's "The Egoist."
3.   Billy Collins's "Silence."
4.   Judy Brown's "The Piñata."
5.   "Las Chavas," a prose piece by Spencer Reece, in *Poetry Magazine*: https://www.
poetryfoundation.org/poetrymagazine/articles/detail/70185.
6.   Yusef Komunyakaa's "Envoy to Palestine."
7.   James Wright's "A Blessing."
8.   Jane Kenyon's "Peonies at Dusk."
9.   Chuck Palahniuk's novel, *Survivor*.
10.   Richard Blanco's "The Island Within."

11. An interview with Jennifer Tamayo: http://depauliaonline.com/2015/02/09/artist-jennifer-tamayo-talks-dora-the-explorer-and-dreamers/.

12. Pablo Neruda's "The Men."

13. Teow Lim Goh's "Black Orchid."

14. Rick Barot's "On Gardens."

15. Roberto Harrison's "[4, 2]."

16. Norman Cameron's "Naked Among the Trees."

17. Sandra M. Castillo's "Letter to Yeni on Peering into Her Life."

18. Eavan Boland's "Domestic Violence."

19. Adam Johnson's novel, *The Orphan Master's Son*.

20. Sylvia Plath's "Fever 103°."

21. Chris Abani's "Sanctificum."

22. Sylvia Plath's "Daddy."

23. Britney Spears's song, "Outrageous."

24. Dean Young's "Sean Penn Anti-Ode."

25. Natalie Diaz's "No More Cake Here."

26. Victor Hugo's novel, *The Hunchback of Notre Dame*.

27. Safiya Sinclair's "How to be an Interesting Woman: A Polite Guide for the Poetess."

28. Czeslaw Milosz's "Incantation."

29. Victor Hernández Cruz's "Airoplain."

30. Maurya Simon's "Russell Market."

31. Lee Herrick's "How to Spend a Birthday."

32. Bruce Weigl's "Song of Napalm."

33. Lemony Snicket's *A Series of Unfortunate Events*.

34. Claude McKay's "After the Winter."

35. An interview with C. Dale Young on Divedapper.com: https://www.divedapper.com/interview/c-dale-young/.

36. Edgar Albert Guest's "The Little Orphan."

37. Anne Higgins's "Georgia O'Keeffe Looks Over Her Shoulder."

REBECCA HAZELTON

HOUSING CRISIS

From an aerial view, the cul-de-sacs

                      are a chalk horse,

are bison leaping. People long gone.

The landscape

        makes inroads on the roads,

the outside

sniffs the air, settles in.

Each morning

the robins hop closer

        to the abandoned houses,

        steal hair ties, borrow stuffng

        from the torn recliner,

        while the paper wasp

                adds another ruff of trim to her house,

                and stuffs the tubes with eggs.

                      First published in *THE CINCINNATI REVIEW*

GERAMEE HENSLEY

———

FEEDING CYCLE

Dear fat tongue / rendered out the belly / of a dead god / Dear mobile / of black teeth & stained glass / I am your deliverer / Do not let today's / provisions / be a bullet / down the esophagus / Too much rice / a hail of gunfire / what my cousins & I / call rice clog / Too much rice / casts shadow in a pit / where there shouldn't be shadow / Is there a history / that is not edible? / What about a myth / that ain't crispy? / Before we built boats / the ocean was an excess / of navy gravy / Good God / I have wrecked my body with excess / Dear earthquake magnet / Dear caterpillar cannibalizing / its own egg / arrange / the stretch marks / just right / & you'll have a map / dreaming of water / water / where there shouldn't be water / I am patron saint / of mouth & gut / I have explored foreign worlds / with just my teeth & tongue / O the noshing gnostic / the caustic aquatic / out the rotting faucet / you must change your life / This is what I think / as I eat pizza / topped with bacon / cheddar & fried potato skin / Good God / I have wrecked my body with excess / Dear Rainer Maria Rilke / this / is how / you must approach / a bullet / laughing / & like a bigger bullet

First published in *RAMBUTAN LITERARY*

REBEKAH DENISON HEWITT

———

ELEGY FOR WHAT ALMOST WAS

Days the rain feels like an action verb, I speak,
hear only absence pouring
from my mouth. A waterfall. The closing
of a jewelry clasp
around my neck, like a hand.

A child thinks of dying
as simply
the absence of movement.

The rain feels like it's happening to us.
God's spit, angel tears, answer to some tribal prayer,
to someone saying thank god
we needed the rain. Until river banks swell
into park benches, swallow roads.

It's that kind of excess we are given–

we have so many letters to arrange
into another person's name,
there are whole books about it.

The naming protects nothing.

God hands you a silver tray of letters.
When you reach for them,
he jerks the whole shining thing back.

A baby dies inside a mother
while the coffee shop down the street
gives away free drinks on its anniversary.
Everyone walks out smiling and into the valley

of this death and all the others.
The living left in the failures
of language and prayer. I tell my son too much.

Back from preschool
we drive past the cemetery.
A blur of yellow, red flowers, his voice
from the backseat, saying "mom,
how do we take off our bodies?"

First published in *THE COLUMBIA POETRY REVIEW*

CATHERINE JAGOE

ARCTICA ISLANDICA

1.

Seeing the ice, congealing like white fat
on the dark stock of the pond, I think
of the four-hundred-and-five-year-old clam
just dredged from the Arctic Ocean
north of Iceland. Quahog *Arctica Islandica*,
the oldest living creature ever found,
born the year the English landed on Cape Cod
and William Shakespeare wrote *Othello*,
three when *Don Quixote* hit the press,
seven when Galileo peered through
his first-ever telescope. In those cold
and pristine seas it drifted, larval, landed
upon velvet silt and burrowed in,
growing a film of shell a year. Daily,
it sipped a slow rain of plankton.
Global warming researchers from Wales
sawed, unsuspecting, through its small,
drab and unremarkable shell to tell
its age, counting its rings like a tree's.
An unfortunate aspect of our work
was that the clam died.

2.

I once worked eight years in the deep
Midwest at a job I hated, in a town known only
for the invention of barbed wire and GM corn.

The Chicago and Northwestern Railroad ran
right through it. Freight trains
woke me at ungodly hours, wailing
like banshees, long into the seamy night,
shaking the floorboards and the raddled
window sashes in the clapboard houses.

3.
The last glacier of the last
Ice Age passed through the city
I live in now, scouring all beneath.
Just west of here, it stopped.
The country beyond has hilltops,
views, variety, a sense of perspective.
To us, the glacier bequeathed the shriven plain,
the sand and clay I wrestle with
each summer, planting annuals.
Ten thousand years have passed
and still, this far north, winter
is a spiritual exercise, weight-
training for the soul.

4.
The Roto-Rooter Man tries doggedly
but fails to fix the trammeled drain.
He blames it on the trees,
their greedy roots. Sober
for twelve years, he says,
he's gone back to the drink.
Was it the blizzard? I think,
the freezing rain?

Too many drains?
After that visit he vanishes,
answers no more calls.

5.

My son, five, wants to know
why God, who could choose to make us
live forever, lets us die.
It's not kind of him, he reasons, puzzled,
beginning to be aggrieved.

6.

I know Tylenol and temperatures and loose teeth.
I know mounds of corn snow and blebbed ice.
I know whitegraybrown.
I know Christmas lights
in the dark. I know
chapped lips.

7.

A ten-year-old in Mexico
glues his hand to the bedstead
after Christmas, not wanting
the humdrum life of school.

8.

That clam and I have things in common:
the drabness of our lives,
the cold, the hidden muscle.
I am reminded of him when the snows
keep falling and I weep over onions,
endlessly load the dishwasher,
endlessly wipe the counters with a dirty cloth,

do endless laundry and find underpants
and fix holes in knees. As I clean
cat vomit and hairballs.
Contemplate my small living room,
endlessly choked by toys.

I know thickened.
I know a slowed heart.
I know hunger expanding.

9.
I want marigolds and mangoes.
I want lambs keeping me awake
with their bawling and celandines
on old airfields and the valleys opening.
I want woods full of bluebells.
I want the mountains of North Wales:
Moel Siabod, Cadair Idris, Tryfan.

I want figs and custard apples.
I want thyme on the hillsides
and lemons on the trees.
I want to go back to that place in Spain
called "Birth of the River World."

I want a Welsh men's choir
with a thunderous golden organ
to fell me, belting out "Cwm Rhondda"
like the crowds at rugby matches:
Bread of Heaven, Bread of Heaven,
Feed me till I want no more (want no more)
Feed me till I want no more.

10.

I open and inhale saffron, desiring
everything to be yellow, orange, red.
All winter, I cook foods from abroad.
Fry olive oil, turmeric and sweet paprika,
sweat shallots. I cook basmati,
brown rice, purple, white. Roast squash
in oil of French hazelnuts
till carmelized. Grate ginger root.
Split green cardamom, pour
coconut milk. Chop feta cheese
and dill. Simmer broth
of miso, shiitake, kelp.

11.

I listen to the shipping forecast
for the British Isles:
Dogger, Fisher, Viking, German Bight,
Rockall, Shannon, Fastnet, Lundy,
Irish Sea. South wind veering west later,
gale force eight, occasional showers, rain.

12.

Growing up near Wales, I never listened
to Welsh men's choirs. I only noticed
how barren and poor the life was:
rain on slate roofs, slag heaps,
the mountains bleak and shrouded.
I never noticed with what joy
they could sing of hardship,
ordinariness, endurance.

I never expected
Happiness, pilgrim
in this barren land.
This barren, rich life.
Our unremarkable existences,
with their secret, iridescent insides.

First published in *BLOODROOT*

MARLIN M. JENKINS

———

ODE TO MY UNI-BROW

Perhaps it is not pronounced enough to easily notice,
at least from a distance, but praise be to the hairs
populating the Bering Strait, or more accurately

crossing the Mediterranean—bridge like cedar planks
with black nails, bridge like the boat
my jido came here in, bridge to Dearborn,

Michigan. The hairs stand up like spines, like each
is a monument over the bridge
of my nose. Since high school I used to keep the middle

trimmed, used clippers to separate such striving
for togetherness, in the name of neatness, I told myself,
though how so many of us have tried to pass, and true—

that is a form of survival but this now also
a form of thriving, of what refuses to be cut down
any longer, so praise be to the hairiness my Lebanese

family shares, praise be to owning what may keep
the TSA's eyes on us, though god-willing not their hands
(and fuck the TSA, while we're at it), and praise be

to pride and to the Muslim man at the gas station
who asks if I am Muslim, too, and though I am not, praise
to being seen as a brother (and to the beard

and back and knuckle hair, while we're at it)—
an oak with so many of its leaves
refusing to enter another shaven autumn,

a cedar holding tight to all its needles.

First published in *WAXWING*

MARK KRAUSHAAR

————

MIDAS

I buy this Crown Vic on the cheap,
no back seat, blown shocks, shot springs so
I fix it up and flip it and I'm up two large
when everything I touch turns gold.

It's autumn
and I'm watching the trees
bend together in perfect accord.
I can't lose at the ponies, I'm winning at slots:
new truck, bass boat, trip to Spain and then, strange,

leaving for school my daughter turns into a statue, gold
but, still, a statue—first her face and hands
and then her hair and anymore I don't go anywhere,
I don't touch anything or anyone and my wife
stands alone at the sink as though,
beyond the gold and the cars
and the cash, love itself is not enough.

It's autumn
and I'm watching the light-buoyed leaves
rise up and bow down with a subtle complicity.

First published in *HUDSON REVIEW*

C. KUBASTA

DESIRING, WITH EMBEDDED TANKAS

I had a boyfriend once, who believed in Decomposition. We swerved
his truck to each hummock of roadkill, careening back roads, finishing
the work of some come-before traveler, flattening carcasses into
unrecognizability. Less for the highway crew, he'd say. They're already
dead, he'd say. Returning them to nature. Some things just are, "belief" is
not the right word, verbed or

not. Common egrets, / known as the Great White Heron / gather at the
maw / of the stream that feeds the lake, / too many too count. I thought /

them solitary birds. I had a boyfriend once, who wouldn't sleep with
me. He didn't believe in latex, artificial hormones, the calendar or his
own control. I can't, he said, risk bringing a life into this world I'm not
prepared to care for. I'd plead for skin, sheathed in multiple prophylactics,
only succeed

occasionally. / At certain times, lakeflies clot / the air, thrumming, their /
mouthless bodies. My body / hungers, vibrates engines with /

no discernible center. I have a friend who careens between dark places;
imagines his beloved with secret lives & loves or the girl of his dreams,
placid and perfect and untouched. He snares along the creek bed in
season, returns to red flags

awave. To harvest / a turtle, you'll need a tub / to trap the blood. So /
much blood, an oil-slick, pooling. / But the meat is tender, caught /

between clades. On the river road to work, two cars ahead the driver clips a squirrel, and the wind catches its body, wiffling the stunned creature aloft, little kite. As I approach it makes for the side of the road, dragging

the weight of itself / with front paws extended, taut. / I should square the tires / and end the animal pain / but the body wants its wants.

First published in BURNT DISTRICT

JOSH LEFKOWITZ

———

WHEN THE LOBSTER GROWS

The thing I don't like about Lexapro is that it makes it hard to feel the bad feelings. This is also what I like most about Lexapro. May I tell you a story about the lobster? When the lobster grows, ecdysis occurs. Ecdysis is another word for shedding (this is allowed, by the way—you can explain a word for the reader's sake—I love to help the reader—I live to help the reader). Well, so, the lobster grows—all through its life, actually— and thus he is constantly molting forward, out of his former home and towards new ones. But the time in which the lobster shifts from a smaller shell to a larger shell is the most vulnerable, and thus, it must remain hidden for seven to fourteen days. I have been taking Lexapro for approximately twenty-one months now, which is approximately seventeen days in lobster time, according to a law of nature that I just made up. What I'm saying is, I'm beginning to grow more curious about the dark brown hues from before—were they really so bad? The thing I don't like about Lexapro is that I wonder about all the other shells that might be waiting for me, out where the water is choppy and cold, if only I'd be brave enough to dive. The thing I like most about Lexapro is how it keeps me alive.

First published in *DECEMBER MAGAZINE*

ISSA M. LEWIS

———

DETROIT

Toothless and sullen, the old cat skulks
along the fence.

It is a piece of work, this night
with its sliver moon and smog.

The density of the sky is crushing
the neighborhood like empty beer cans,
the roofs sagging down deep into the joints.

This is a place nobody stops, visible
from the highway but ripped away without ceremony,
a bit of circumstance, no exit.

And isn't there anything here
not worth a 20-gallon garbage barrel?

Inside the homes without doors
or windows, is there anything unburnt?
A tongue of char was here, licking

its way around corners, waving to the night
as it feasted on dry rot. They're not homes now,
weren't even before that.

They were when Diana Ross cooed
baby love, my baby love

and cars were made of metal and sweat,
the strongest amalgam. Every man went
into that furnace and came out with keys.

Nothing felt fragile. Fingernails were meant
to be dirty and skin was supposed to be scarred
and upon those small sacrifices they built their homes.

Where have you gone, Woodward Avenue?
There are weeds in your teeth.

Who would have thought lives could be crumpled
like sheets of paper? That a bottle thrown
through a window could ignite a Molotov cocktail

of boiling blood, that paint on a brick wall
could bring down the whole thing?
But not everyone left with gravel in their shoes.

Some of them are still here.
Someone's got to feed that cat, after all.

First published in *BLUE LYRA REVIEW*

D. A. LOCKHART

———

EAST SAGINAW STREET
AND THE LANSING THAT SHALL BE YOURS

Night plays out through Kennedy
Kush on the car radio, green aural
lighting puddles on empty sidewalks,
sparsely filled wide boulevards
passed at a steady forty-five miles
per hour. Side streets give birth
to long rows of tall trees, cars
parked in promise for the people
and homes you can't see. For
the speed, for the depth of night,
for the wide dispersal of light
from scraggly utility poles, it plays
as if these moments are off-channel
late night on a discarded movie set,
left open for you to dream up
a Midwestern city you would want.
So it is, this night, in this city shall
become yours as you speed to its
outskirts for an all-night superstore
and little things, cellophane fruit,
Old Spice, and day-old bread loaves,
in the only places left for you to claim.

First published in *TWYCKENHAM NOTES*

———

THE RUTS

Most have been plowed up or paved over
but you can still find them, tracks cut
    deep into the earth by prairie schooners
crossing that great green ocean, pitching
    waves of pasture out where there's nothing
else to do but live. Concealing their detritus—
    a piece of sun-bleached buffalo skull, a button
from a cavalry soldier's coat—the ruts wind
    their way beneath leafy suburban streets, lie
buried under a Phillips 66 and the corner
    of a Pizza Hut where a couple sits slumped
in their booth. Yet here and there, like a fish
    head breaking the surface of the water, they
emerge in a school teacher's back yard or a
    farmer's field, evidence of wagons packed
with hardtack and hard money, thousands of
    draft animals tended by traders with blistered
feet, their journey both bleak and romantic.
    That's the kind of proof I like, a scar I can put
my hand to, history that will dust my fingers
    with a little bit of suffering, a little bit of bone.

First published in *THIRD COAST*

CHARLES MALONE

———

ONE DOZEN FROZEN PONDS

three kids ring the white pondering the designs of water
in time, the beautiful girl will find out she is beautiful
the troubled golden boy will find out he is troubled
the third is the last to follow across the ice
he hears a warning echo in bone and falls through

millions of boys must fall through frozen ponds
they freeze and become non-persons filling up
the space below the ice above the water

instant thaw clean ice to algae bloom
solid then soup

to you through the ice golden and beautiful
troubled and knowing

mothers to strip us down to long johns
and worry us warm in the tub
and then gone

woven clove grove fro froguth zen
muslin doe plimb would bracken burnt bough
bow oxen was bought own wonder wanter
well wood wild coarse coursing curse

into a gasp of feathers

First published in *SALTFRONT*

ION

for Tracy K. Smith and Roger Reeves

It's a beautiful day
in America and we
are all waiting for
something terrible to happen.

A girl's balloon pops
on the commuter train
and we think it
is a gunshot.

The leaves we pass
sparkle with imaginary
dew. More people hold
books in their hands

than I have ever seen.
At the poetry reading
you discussed
lynchings in Paradise.

On this beautiful
suburban day,
all I can see is
lucid unease

once we've talked about
death, a feathered
final breath of the higher
self, unstable, seeing.

First published in *RIVER STYX*

JOHN McCARTHY

SAME OLD STORY

All the names spray-painted at the base of the abandoned silo—
they weren't ours. It was harvest season and beneath the sky
the tenor of fall sounded like rocks thrown at its side—
a dirge. There was a hitch in your step as we walked
through the wheatgrass looking for a spot to be alone. The wind
was picking up like it always does when telling this story,
and it felt like having a flat tire on the side of a dirt road
a long way from anywhere. In those moments I know
exactly what I want or what I don't want. One or the other.
There's nothing to do around here, you said. I nodded,
but I'm not really sure what I meant by nodding. We listened
to a weathervane sway. It sounded like rust. Or it was a gate
opening and closing, slamming its lift-latch. I didn't know
you smoked, but you stubbed a cigarette out in the dirt
and flicked it away. I was spinning a pinecone in my hands.
You know how it goes. It felt familiar. Then it changed.

First published in *ZIN DAILY*

JOHN McCRACKEN

———

THE WAFFLE HOUSE INDEX,
or IF THE WAFFLE HOUSE IS CLOSED
THE POPULACE IS SHRINKING

But the signs are still on and the coffee is still brewing.
There is a solace in the buzzing of the local news channel.

I listen to trees uproot themselves to the key of eggs cracked
on the open grill and doubt that these walls could fall.

I didn't think myself in the presence of a refuge until
the night we sat on the hillside and peered through its windows.

You sat close to me and I cried for the first time in a while
and you soaked up my proximal grief, a syrup weighing you down.

Somehow our view into the diner from that Kentucky motel
made me laugh and cheer at the thought of the lives on the inside.

We weaved stories about how the waitress had always been
        beautiful
and the truckers that kept their bellies full and minds sharp.

When I picture the end of the world with all of its trauma spread
across the landscape, I see highways cracking open and forests

scorched by the grace of God and wind speeds that could snap my
spine in half but I hear a jukebox still playing and our lives are
    something

infinite and non-perishable, and there is always a seat for me at this
    table.

First published in *PANOPLY*

MICHAEL MLEKODAY

———

SELF-PORTRAIT, WEARING BEAR SKULL AS MASK

The world looks like fangs.
You look like fangs to the world.
Everything is quieter
so you shout, slang and other language
coming out warbled and hungry
as a barbed arrow.
The world does not care what you eat
so long as it is not them,
but motherfuck, they all look ripe
from the inside of a mouth.
The mouth is a cave and you are the fire
within, or you are the cave painting,
the ghost of something slain by something larger,
or the mouth is the scope of a rifle
and you are a boy away from home.
You are a boy in the shape of animal
and in the dark, everything feels like the woods.
The sweat, the fresh smack of spring
brings blood to your face
but you are still just skull and imagined claw
to the world, just the dumb perfect body
of death. You stopped speaking long ago.
You haven't eaten yet today,
and the world looks bright as winter.

First published in *THE DEAD ANIMAL HANDBOOK*

SIMONE MUENCH & DEAN RADER

———

IN DARK ACCIDENTS THE MIND'S SUFFICIENT GRACE

First Line By Delmore Schwartz

In dark accidents the mind's sufficient grace
is like the moment in a song when
the cello rows in on its tiny boat
of light. We need a word for survival
in nerve time, in cell time, before the world
limps off with our belongings, before our
lips are sewn shut, and we are sentenced for
pulling back the black curtains of history.

The past has rinsed off the apophantic
and slipped into the to-be-able-to-be.
Its nails are painted, its knives are oiled
as it warriors up for the apocalyptic
release of dissonant notes through icy
gallows, crafting hymns for the newly condemned.

First published in *GHOST TOWN*

CHRISTOPHER NELSON

———

COCK FIGHT

Being, as a general rule, left-handed, the blade is fitted
     to the right claw of the largest rooster to counterbalance
     the benefit of its greater strength, and the higher jumper
     gets a half-inch blade instead of the usual three-quarters:
     death and the desire for symmetry

through asymmetry. The Romans employed similar methods
     in the Colosseum: a man advantaged by horseback
     wore a blackout helmet; a frail prisoner struggled
     with a heavy sword while his Herculean opponent
     wielded a shield small as a salad plate.

When I was younger, identity and sexuality were more
     ensnared, and discrepancies in physicality heightened arousal:
     a swollen phallus beside a limp inferior, a six-foot athlete
     and a scrawny boy surrendering to him on the carpet.
     As one ages, a paradox becomes familiar:

the increased distance between present and past may not weaken
     the influence of what was: a child still resides inside
     the wrinkling man; a child still runs through pastures,
     nearly convinced that belief alone can make him soar,
     so thin is the separation between dream and non-dream.

Isn't the acceptance that there is such a thing as non-dream
     what marks the descent into adulthood? Before battle
     the cocks are made furious by a lesser bird called
     "the monkey," then they fight—leaping and fluttering,
     feathers flaring, ebony, emerald, and rust—until one dies.

In the golden eyes, bewitching calm. When I was ten or eleven,
        an errand sent me to the high school, a mission of retrieval,
        a folder for a teacher. There was a "secret" landing
        at the top of the stairs by the unused dance studio,
        a six-by-ten-foot sanctuary for those who cut class.

My wrong turn led me there, where I watched, unnoticed
        for half a minute, four boys—two I recognized from
        the wrestling team—flaps of blue jeans opened, shirts
        half removed or pulled up and held in teeth, tanned torsos,
        taut nipples, tight curls from navels down to the red rods

being thrummed as one counted *twenty-three, twenty-four,*
        twenty-five—a contest: who can come the quickest—
        twenty-six, twenty-seven, twenty-eight and the pearlescent
        spit from one, the others surprised by the speed—
        flushed cheeks and *Jesus*, a soft exclamation.

One saw me then, and he fixed my eyes with a fierce intensity,
        not anger or desire, not fear or shame, but perhaps
        some feeling that contained all of these. Their age
        and audacity granted them power over me.
        I fled, returned without the folder,

said I couldn't find it, and nothing else was asked. So this is a story about
        introjection, the imprinting of consciousness by events
        charged with symbolic force. I don't know how many times
        I've revisited the top of the stairs in my mind.
        Like all birds, the cock has little blood, but a bleeding wound

won't make them stop, the desire to fight not quelled by injury;
        instead the organism persists in its aggression until
        failure, death-lust still active when the body

is unable to respond. In high school I had a secret lover.
When he would enter me, what I marveled at most was how

who I was—or thought I was—would fade,
    a much easier way to lose the self, I used to muse,
    than crawling for miles on hands and knees,
    like the pilgrims I read about, to a holy altar, where,
    in the body's exhausted distress, what seems to be

—and may in fact be—the soul leans outward, through the eyes,
    toward the material. I was wrong, my metaphor incomplete.
    An erasure of and a heightening of the sense of self
    have the same outcome. As the blade is affixed to the foot,
    the master will whisper, and the cock feels not the meaning

of the words, but its god's desire. It has been said that
    the contest is not between the birds but the souls
    of their keepers. And some day, too, I will realize
    that this extended comparison I've been making
    also fails, as when a young man, who seeks

in the bodies of others the virility possessed in his own,
    comes to know that he is and is not his father
    —image of two teetering scales—as he erroneously
    believes that in coming there is a kind of knowing,
    so he comes and comes and comes, as we all do—or did—

for our various reasons, in our various seasons, watched over,
    we might sense, by an intelligence there is no name for—
    like the roosters, the audience invisible to them, beyond
    their cognition, despite the necessity of its presence
    in the bloodletting that defines them.

First published in *BLOOM*

HOWL

For Toni Keller

I saw the best minds of my generation destroyed by wedding planners,
    dieting, in shapewear,
dragging themselves in cute outfits through the freezer section for the
    semifreddo bender,
blessed innovative cloister girl pin-ups burning to know the rabbi of
    electricity in poverty, obedience, in the dream stick of opium and the
    green Wi-Fi fuse,
who marveling and cramping and wired and allergic lock themselves out of
    their apartments in the trenchant imperfect delight of early day,
who bared their minds to bar friends by the train in twilight and saw tiny
    figures like fireflies splendoring apartments Botoxed flat like canvas,
who passed through universities with sensual indulgence addicts devoted
    to the indefinite space of maps and science labs while the committees
    shifted paperwork,
who left the university from a numbing homesickness for the rez and the
    old alcoholic lover family father temper crack methamphetamine
    birdsong,
who galvanized in excitable need and microdermabrasioned took the
    lonely exit ramp on the nature, constitution, and forces of matter,
who failed their enzyme multiplied immunoassay technique not once
    but more than once because some guy came into her room talking
    about publishing, hash and vintage cardigans, drunk to the
    abdominals looking for speed crank coke & codeine,
who took Molly and mint and Motrin and methaqualone naked in the
    unhappy light of *Saved by the Bell* on the hotel flat screen,

with spring of 1924 beautiful imaginary wheat stalk wanderlust
nylons travelhope,

not allowed to explore alleys or ride the rails or hitchhike either because of
the magnetic pink and with all the years of training spread out
boundless the rules and safety tiresome before them,

Paradise papery Wisconsin-Madison visionary blue green crosshatched
for elevation maps baked wild open unspoiled lands of Lake Kivu &
Congo, ardent delirious combustible desire to go astray rove stir
evolve princesslike,

who busted out against parents' wishes clattered cross-county in a Model
T with another girl to see the iron pyrite fool's gold The West and the
finally wide open-legged Pacific zones,

who wrote letters anyway to old boyfriends before setting out on the
breathless orange high desert confusion with gold carrying canvas
buckets for the extra water for the car,

who talked all night in the tourist camps and were up with the sun and
snappish with hunger,

the navigators in terror of the steep mountain road refreshing the radiator
with water inhaling the rust steam fragrance of open road red oxygen
metal and a lunar happiness,

whistlingsinging bowwowing mooing at the glamorous elations of altitude
and the hayburner no handcuff no hush money open whangdoodle
fiery western sky deposits of gold and silver lost stories gun-toting
candlemaking dance hall prostitute stowaway freedoms not to
mention ball bang bareback gamahuche cowboy,

who listened while the mechanic romanced over velocity and atonement
die-stampings on sheet steel and drop forgings while the diner
waitress ground out pies and pies and pies,

wandering nylons suffering while the word of engagements and new babies
began its bone descent by mother's phrasing and martini lunch date
with the old school of the hot comb and the inner ear,

who broke up with boyfriends and walked tap heels on streets for dentist's
appointment a doctor's appointment an interview a newspaper
grocery dinner tomato,

who found the sublet which for what she was making she could
afford but the roommate had trouble with rent alarm clock rooster
cock boyfriend,

who saw her clothing was available in size 00 so it was time to disappear
entirely,

who took a job selling print invitations to promoters where the desk was
dusty with coke Aunt Mary Aunt Nora Aunt Hazel and also dust,

who took the cab to the Upper West Side to deliver the express mail
package of rocks and rocks of powder for the boss in his high-
ceilinged mirrored walls, comatose blonde sylph and suits of bright
licorice acrylic fibers,

who watched the mistress arrayed in pelts panther drunk and ringed with
minerals achieving her highest human form,

who leaving in the elevator sad at her scuffed boots of the underclass felt
the mirror reflection of her mother repeating little lamb who made
thee dost thou know,

who considered the elevator's speculum dilating her cataract radioscope
telescope manifestation,

who listened to the *TODAY* show while she Kindled exasperated on an
exercise bike in the new pink Manhattan Island 22.7 square miles of
dawn,

who carried her infant in a baby sling she designed herself out of thrift
store fabrics,

who wept because *caesarean* was a term for last resort, having felt cheated
by the dictionary of the pain of real meaning and deliverance of child
into atmosphere,

who anyway flamed ardent and breathless in illuminated swinging as
she sang lulling smooth neurons already waddling inside the
babygirl's palimpsest brain,

who watched the girl with highlights blow her boyfriend and then blew her
boyfriend and then copulated analytically with a stranger waiter
painter truck driver in a sorcery of forgetfulness,

who philosophized in the meadow flowers on her back to the sound of
black flies stirring the leaves and let herself be touched by the rude
one so she could see the show without paying and lost that beautiful
little gold earring she'd never see the likes of it again,

who contemplated such disappointments again for the tenth time the
twentieth thirtieth time the earrings whooshing the Cleopatra
shouldered sighs the exchange while everywhere boys are having sex
and playing basketball afterward and laughing,

who is up nights and days peeing restlessly endlessly with nothing but
cranberry cranberry cranberry eucharist for the body's
unyielding sciences and the UTI of the Punishing Boy God who
decided who wins,

who felt the embryo always crunching futures with crushing weight of the
fixed decree by which the laws of the universe are prescribed the
bitch of necessity the bitch of chance and the DNA overlord,

who drove her two babies wild into the lake to what she imagined was
whiteness,

who from curiosity and an old curse tried the spinning wheel in the coldest
room of the castle and spilled drops of blood on the snow, fell into a
sleep that would last a hundred years, until, what else, a boy kisses
her,

who lost her virginity to the three bad playing cards in cardboard plastic
coated false love the slippery wet Jack of Text Messages the forcible
Jack of All Fours the odd can opener of need filled by the One-Eyed
Jack who finally demystifies though it turns out not only slightly
painful but truly unpleasant, followed by all the new information,

who tore at it with an honest brutal mad need stripping herself this once
of the manicure of propriety and sweetheart headband of the high
school dance for his long-form journalism of a cock and ferocious

butcher meat smell,

who blonde as a lit match in Denver watched him enter and stare and
took the stare not seeing yet inside the iris a splash of sweetened road
that turned with pills magic grass breasts bridge rooftop roadside
bedside blindside shenanigans honey,

who took iconic photographs on her Brownie camera recording two myths
across the street from her house, arms around each other, C.C.,
secret hero of this poem, lover and marble statue muse, hot Dickens
reader — props to the memory of her innumerable pots of spaghetti
while the boys with shining minds could wander at night,

who blonde as an aristocrat felt him watch her withhold her soft
imaginative thighs while another guilty child bride tumbled sweet on
a trampoline it was intoxicating,

who fell deeply for his car thief master love railroad seducer inhaled the
marvelous heartbeat divine heat broke fed it and waited like the road
was a closed door to the doctor's office and Russell Street the
anteroom of creation and love before it went mad haywire, if it ever
would,

who made cacciatore with the chickens used in the Payne Whitney Clinic
trials because they were 14 cents a pound,

who tired of Sheila and the Upper East Side waiting for revolution among
porcelain and jumped out/through/out the window to mainline all
seven stories, literally broke the window she wanted out that much,

who suffering as a muse in the limestone of ancient outlandish Tangier
may have believed in God but even so wasn't going to discuss it with a
bop poet on the telephone,

who hymned the confusing magnetic pink lozenge and painted whore
bluesy blue-note secret-love-note whole-note half-note passages
bellydancing gentle hip sliding doumbek thrum belly counterpoint
shimmyshimmywhimseyfuck,

who skirted her soul's furnishings in the lazar house of man poetics, its
closets filled with vests and ties,

who imprisoned for apostasy chained up delivered the child squallish and
    reddening into the ballot of time,

who studied painted photographed, raised children and pined, bought
    kreplach & Whopper Jrs dreaming of three square
    family kingdom of the push mower and powdered milk,

who rode the welfare road trip of pouring innumerable thermoses of coffee,
    feeling the freedom wind-in-your-hair of wrapping sandwiches in
    wax paper,

who studied and prayed and wrote in diaries and platinumed hair gleamed
    gloved hands stewed rabbit in blood and wine like a priest and shot
    the baby out in blood over everything,

who worked stable and domestic and artful and innovative and sacrificed
    nothing, fig trees excitedly massively blossoming not that one that
    disappointed Jesus for not ripening,

who star-spangled lost in her housebound Eden cursed with orchards and
    a million gossipy daffodils, writing & nursing & not on the lists as he
    dipped a pen quite elsewhere repeatedly, crying purring the distance
    openmouthed,

who burned her novel this actually happened destroyed a second *Bell Jar*
    dedicated to him call her impossible but the leap from it must have
    been split-second maddening rapturous,

who blew him three times and then his friend because it was hard to say no
    when you say no nobody likes you as much when you say yes or even
    whatever you are loved into momentary relevance existence,

who begged twenty dollars from each friend to pay for a secret abortion, her
    man needing the child but not her to show his father manliness by
    imperialism of the womb and eventual abandonment like any
    suburban mall,

who protested the clinic shouting who themselves got abortions at that
    same clinic (they had to, don't tell their husbands) came back and
    then protested again for the unborn (but they can't afford another

child) but it should be illegal for the poor, this article was in *Esquire*
of all places, America where is your logic,
who stained the host's linens mad crimson lipstick boy-crazy stigmata
her animal flesh gash her crown of suburban thorns completely
honest about need,
who sketched the body tangible medical painted portraits and lived inside,
who should have been on the road but for the uterus repeatedly
renewing its lease convincing energy affirmative right honey that's
right honey right there,
who gave a light touch delicate hand beautiful chisel cheek blonde wave
Mother Image Madwoman chick and ignu driving inward toward an
isolated, lonely peace,
who brewed serious coffee during the murder and scrambled eggs while
disposing of the body, the detective as best man and
silence thereafter, still unpublished,
who hid his shoes hating to but still he left her for Colt 45 malt liquor
Johnnie Walker Falstaff Beer,
and lived the biography filled however with biographies of the others for
which she made a home flashbulbed in silver their likenesses and
tried love in living room, attic, slanted redeemable love their fingers
articulated like saints,
who after the understandable and recognizable desire loveshape would
then expand, against his will and this was a shame, this lie
abandonment anger congenital analgesia against hope plan bugout
for ten years,
returning in her saffron clothes her flat dimension the mother saint
devotion song of spiritual angers lovingly pressed into an incense
cone of spirituality, her image carved by apostles among the lonely
goat forgotten sheep infant in cozy rags framed by any window to be
honored in her eternal loneliness,
Amherst's Evergreens' First Congregational's cupola and conservatory

hothouse echoing pure song and archway and hymnal
restraint, Daisy who bends her smaller life to his in her fenced-in field
within which the horse can gallop wildly as she likes, grieve her your
best girl
with a still, restrained, almost annoyed sigh, what voice in what
wilderness, minutest cricket, most unworthy flower I will never be
tired — I will never be noisy I will be your best little girl —
nobody else will see me, but you — but that is enough — limitlessness,
wilt thou say,
ah, ladies, good night, good night, good night ladies —
and who therefore know the biology of the soft matter and the cluster of
creation in its salty stellar lonely archive is matched by the sweet
violence of thought,
who transubstantiated across the desert with both of them finally under
the deep clear her blonde beauty and the celestial betrayals arrayed
stellar, Andromeda chained naked to a rock, the Pleiades shedding to
doves to stars,
to recreate young artists' castling brains over the mountain's whelp of
monks in open out-of-bodies absolute ascent,
the madgirl and saint unrecognized and writing madrigal in bedroom and
recipe in library and songs during class and sketching
sunflowers for what's left of us,
and remains magnified sanctified we should be allowed Yitgadal
v'yitkadash sh'mei raba Acanthus whorled and dense and impossibly
real multiplying in fields an abundance of sunflowers serious beauty,
with blooming, ridiculous with blooming, arriving and opening in endless
profusion forever.

First published in *POETRY*

OLATUNDE OSINAIKE

―――

TO RELAY RACE

100m –

reciting my name / accent non-refundable / feels like imported
goods illegal / i grip / clumsy / damn near nauseous
from collateral / a glass boomerang / trembling / the heat
shuffling / in rich gloom / before the caveat collects / exchange

200m –

usually the anonymous / annotates my chin / with their razor
sharp cinch / my jawline / a dirty paradox / reigning adopted
from the sky / the clouds coy / before tapered tongues
twist thorough / revealing only / this brown bittersweet / i brave

300m –

inclusion isn't retribution / the sweat subsides / softly / no need to thank
a tyro who loves / lukewarm first / puzzling after / the palm's swift
embrace / maybe the technique / hypnotizes the hell / out of comfort
to walk / into the chaos / like spiders & black boys

400m –

last night / a native hummed / a negro spiritual / eavesdropping
on my nihilistic / coded prayer / i insist / or vent
as those on air / veil the gist / of prejudice / shameless
so dignified / as if / this is an aviary & i am still / here

First published in *APOGEE JOURNAL*

MATTHEW OLZMANN

———

PHANTOM ROUTES

*A pseudo route or dummy route not associated
with any carrier and programmed on a short
scheme for a holdout.*

—*United States Postal Service,
"Glossary of Postal Terms"*

One starts near the horizon, another forms at the bottom
of Lake Erie. The route a phantom must follow begins
in a graveyard. Another labors along the length of a canyon.

One carries a satchel full of fog, another
pushes a cart of silence and bandages.

The houses where they arrive are usually abandoned,
sometimes demolished. Still, these couriers trudge onward.
They know what they're doing.

Look outside. What do you see?
A wine bottle bashed across the sidewalk?
A dog chasing a ball? Rain?

One phantom carries envelopes stuffed with whispers.
Another specializes in parcels filled
with ash, pencil shavings, bits of broken alarm clocks.

And who cares if the recipient is nameless,
or exists only in photographs? I've seen these figures
work, and they're the best in the business.

There are things I wanted to say to you, times
when I had no words—love,
I will be swept from this earth, erased—
and if I ever find a way,
these are the only messengers I'd trust.

A scrap of newspaper kicked up by the wind.
Taillights disappearing over the ridge.
A knock on the door when no one's home.

First published in *RALEIGH REVIEW*

MY MOTHER SAYS THE SYRIAN REFUGEES LOOK LIKE TOURISTS

because she has just finished telling the story of our escape
and needs to draw a comparison, return us safely to the
    present,

December 2015, we're back at my sister's childproofed house,
keeping warm by winter sun, central heating, and our
    sweatpants;

because some do: "Ghaith joyfully snapped selfies, the
    Aegean
glimmering in the background. He looked much like a
    tourist,"

suggests the reporter at large in the New Yorker article I read
about one refugee's epic escape from Syria, and think of
    again

when my mother can't make room in our story for more
    people;
because my mother never quite has the right words in
    English,

though to be fair, she said "travelers," and seemed anxious
    after;
because she's not callous, you must understand, just
    protective . . .

In the blue porcelain bowl on the granite top kitchen island
where we gather faithfully around my mother and the story,

there are three balls of white rice shaped like warm eggs,
and a fourth, forming in her hands, being pressed into service

as she recounts making them before, wrapped in banana
        leaves
and secreted inside pockets. These are for my nephew, Aidan,

who loves rice like he loves Cheerios, who will be hungry
once his toy train runs off too many tracks, and who just
        turned

two, around the age I was when we left, a coincidence my
        mother
points to like a storybook illustration . . . It's December 1981.

We're dressed in nice clothes because Christmas Eve is our
        cover.
The cathedral in Bà Rịa is packed. If anyone asks why we're
        out,

we can say we were at Mass. Anyone being the police. The
        locals
of course recognize us. We stop at one of the popular stalls

for fresh sugarcane juice, trying to act normal. The nước mía
tastes unbelievably good. The young woman operating the
    noisy,

shiny contraption calms us, and when she spots the Công an
patrolling out front, insists we sit down and just relax in the
    back.

Our boat is parked at the riverbank behind the road that runs
past the market, hidden by the lush green flags growing
    there.

Our third attempt. The last time we waited and waited
at the designated safe house, but no boat ever showed up.

This time we are wiser. My father, thanks to his credentials
as a former Navy officer and ex re-education camp prisoner,

negotiated to be boat captain, which means we travel for
    free—
my mother, my uncle, my cousin, and me—but also means

he can't stay with us because he must collect more
    passengers
at the bus stop. Say you are devising plans to flee. There's a
    group,

on Facebook, Asylum and Immigration Without Smugglers,
you can trust and rely on. Because to be a refugee, you must
    know

where to go, what routes save time and money, if the sea
    today
or tomorrow is fatally dangerous, if the storm is practically
    over,

what island is best to leave for, what to do if you are stuck
in the middle of the forest, where to cross the border at
    night. . .

We have to wait until nightfall. The moon is our lighthouse.
When the time comes, we start walking towards the river

that will lead us to the sea—at this point in my mother's
    account
a new detail emerges, something small, but not there before:

she loses her sandal like in a fairytale by mistake in the street.
Because she thinks she sees police lights up ahead, she
    panics,

hurries in the dark, heart racing, bare foot sparking the path
to the boat motionless and obscure on the river's black
    mirror . . .

In 1981, the rest of the passengers had to pay two to three
cây vàng, about two to three thousand US dollars then.

I learned that traffickers, in 2014, raised their prices again,
charging at least four thousand dollars to smuggle a Syrian

into Italy. I saw the picture of three-year-old Alan Kurdî
and read one article that tried to describe what his small
        body

looked like washed ashore, "face down, his head to one side
with his bottom slightly up—the way toddlers like to sleep."

Waiting in the boat's hold, the story goes, I won't stop crying.
The alarm of my crying unnerves and endangers everyone.

Because my father is the only one on board who knows how
to pilot the boat and navigate the waters, I am not harmed.

Still, my crying. Incessant, unappeasable, loud as a siren.
My mother doesn't know what to do. She has already fed me

the food she brought. The rice balls, the hard-boiled eggs.
She even tried the sleeping pills. Nothing seems to work.

Though it's risky, she finally carries me up to the deck.
Night air quiets me. Because in my version, her black shawl

covers my head as she hums a song nobody can hear,
all silent, all still, like an island in the Mediterranean.

First published in *NEW ENGLAND REVIEW*

PRACTICE

Autumn. Leaves drip and turn over,
round like the goblet of a thigh torn from its animal.

Daylight folds into creases,
a jumbled marathon of birds strung loosely along
telephone wires
and my hair canvasing light paned across the bed's
worn coverlet.

By dusk I will have imagined that dirt roads
are highways
and the cold steel beams of our trailer
are thick layers of shadow from oak trees
pressed into aluminum beating out the doormats
caked with mud.

Rifle fire in the distance.

The first signs of winter. Your boots
dragging the teeth of rotten corn across this barren field.

> *If I let you nuzzle me,*
> *will you leave the children alone?*

Your hands shake. Bullets clip trees.

I hear them through these thin paper panels
that tremble with your knuckle prints: each near miss,
my cheekbones
flush as a newly skinned hide.

Target panic is a condition caused by trying too hard to hit
your mark;
it can only be cured by a closer range.

Once you met a doe on the path near our home.
You said she didn't move: she wanted you to touch her.

First published in *THE BERKELEY POETRY REVIEW*

BUNNIES

In the hallowed shade of basil and beneath the bower
of beans. What do you mean, to be so softly
ruinous? A puff, still as some mute memory
of illicit gnawing I'd like to forget. The dewy
after-chew of missing lettuce, the abrupt
halt of the tulip stalk, budless. I can forgive
your hunger, but not your choices. In the
straw mulch, I uncover a cuddled squirm of fur, all
eyes squinted shut against the view of my
cruel hesitation. Each ball of bunny nubbled
with ears, paws, nose. And somewhere, growing inside
jaws—teeth. You live this life acutely. Quiet and
aquiver, nibbling against the hawk, the fox, the boot,
the dog—in whose own sharp mouth you seem to sing.

First published in *THE IOWA REVIEW*

PAGE #17 FROM A KOZHIKODE GROCERWOMAN'S DIARY

The woman from the big brown thatched cottage with the
"Spoken English Classes"

Banner outside, stopped by yet again. She wanted pepper.

They've everything within the lawns, except for pepper.

Her big- assed mother in law tended to coffee beans,
jackfruits

and cashew but pepper was bad omen. It reminded her of
death.

She needed pepper for fish molee but you know the thing.

She won't chew the pomfret marrow like I do. She has no clue

About the juices trapped inside the marrow. She'll discard
the skin

And make fillets soaked in coconut milk. I wanted to tell her,

Look at me. I'm pepper. Look at my snake skin, my racy
forehead.

Listen to me when I say kurumulaku, a river

Flows inside of me. Pepper was my ocean, my language

Long before Vasco da Gama came over, with his

Nuisance ships and white- skinned missionaries.

Long before that, pepper was in me. It's nothing special

Like you make it seem. I use it for everything, cook it in

Smoldering coconut oil and curry leaves, drench my hair

In it. For the coal darkness braids, for the sharpness

On my skull.

First published in *SILK AND SPICE ANTHOLOGY*

KAREN RIGBY

———

THE BAR SUIT

House of Dior, 1947

After the war, the wasp-waist returns:
silk civility a flag for romance, buttoned-up jacket

over pleated wool. Dior's vision of flower-like women
is made an armor of glamour. Boning and yardage
dazzle even now, a study in minimalist color

styled with luxe hat and heels.
Who doesn't love the regal, criminal feel
of leather gloves drawn past the wrists,

terrifying in their strictured elegance?
The year an editor crowns Dior's collection
as the New Look, the Doomsday Clock debuts

on the cover of *Bulletin of the Atomic Scientists*.
The hand aims seven minutes to midnight.

Inside meringue and black couture, the spleen
builds its own reactor. The future arrives in leonine
steps. The future pivots—all of us witness—

a magician's wife home from the void
mouthing *It's nothing, nothing.*

First published in FOUNDRY

———

BLUE DOG BLUE DOG

Mid-sentence while teaching
a freshman seminar, a stranger

in a blue dog costume enters.
Blue Dog paces in eerily

without saying a word—
mimes his threadbare mitts

for us to carry-on. I search
the shadowbox of mesh

beneath its battered plastic eyes
for any indication of what's next.

Where an ID card should rest,
an empty plastic case swings.

When Blue Dog speaks,
his voice is crushed gravel:

One time I buried a bone.
I buried a bone, then I dug it up.

A part of me leaves my body.
When it's over, he walks out.

Five days later, an Oregon community
college student shoots his English teacher

and nine others. The gunman says,
I've wanted to do this for years.

First published in *THE STOCKHOLM REVIEW OF LITERATURE*

THE LONG NOW

The sky is a map of questions: *what burns,*
how long, where is the middle without an edge?

You ask & my answers are never enough.
When you were small, we lived by milkthirst

& sleep, outside of time & the shifting blues,
unaware of any world beyond the two of us.

But now, you point upward & every question
bears another: *how bright, how many, can we live*

out there? I warm your hands with mine
& tell you how even stars can be cast out

or mistaken. In the Winter Triangle, the red giant
is Betelgeuse, a runaway in a stellar wake

of heat & wind, & soon to supernova.
Just above the pines is the evening star,

which is also the morning star, & not a star
at all, but a cloudy planet, double-seen,

so close to us. Imagine me in Ohio
and you on the ocean, a pole to the other

in half-dark, where the strongest light
is Venus, low in opposite skies.

Why is it not all one day you ask
& I cannot answer because all I want

is more of your days. If each life is a single
spoken sentence, then I know how yours

begins, but will never hear it whole.
All the time & we do not have time. I draw

a circle split in two. The empty curve is half
a turn, a door, or a burial mound, the way

my body without me is an outline of moss.
I could tell you how distant light from stars

still finds us long after they burn out,
or that bones are made of their dying dust

but that is no consolation. We are experts
at division. You want to know *how far,*

where we go, & what happens after.
To locate ourselves is to measure separation

from another. We are in the same field
but forty years apart, a thousand feet

above the sea, & five hundred miles
from the graves of my grandparents.

Listen, my love, the universe cannot
be fathomed, not with circles of stone,

an abacus, or even a telescope. If infinity
is edgeless, then the center becomes wherever

we are. You are my fixed point as we spin
on an axis, turn in orbits inside of orbits,

& speed outwards. Instead of a sentence,
may our lives be endless questions. On Venus,

each day is longer than a year, & if we keep
walking toward the sun, it will never be night.

First published in *TERRITORY*

MAX SCHLEICHER

———

PIGGSVILLE

Crossed wet and coal-grinning. Flood land
traced back three generations. Black spores
pattern tavern wrists. The gasping
light in chill hands. The convicts scraping
finish from basement steps. I drop
from porch tables to diving black swifts
at Falk Corporation. Light unable
to swallow is their flight comfortable
in my own skin.
I get it right, this light I remember so cruelly in.
Believe one thing I say, that this is my bread:
three boys spit in my face and break my ribs.
It's my life to steal what's theirs, so I give,
gather myself by the neck to show you
a common dream of low houses looks back.

First published in *UP NORTH LIT*

CHEMISTRY

From the middle Dutch *boele*, which
    means lover, *bully* was a term
of endearment in the sixteenth century,
    which meant that a feudal lord
could take the hand of his love
    under the apple trees in spring
and exclaim: *my bully*, feeling
    adrenaline flood his body as his heart
rate tripled and his palms began
    to release water mixed with urea,
ammonia, salt. Essentially,
    he could feel what I felt over four
centuries later when Ian Starkey
    called me a fag. I was fourteen,
and the next day he kicked me twice,
    spat in my face, took my glasses
and wouldn't give them back.
    And the whole time sweat glands
were developing in our armpits and genitals,
    and our adrenals were releasing
corticosteroids, and something
    about testosterone was why, though
I hated him, I kept imagining
    him with his shirt off. True,
Ian Starkey knew how to hurt me,
    but I doubt he knew why he was doing it

or that we feel pain when neurons
     in the brain convert an electrical
signal to a chemical signal and back
     again, which is also what allows
us to feel a kiss or my brain
     to take strange comfort imagining
all the boys of the world leaning into
     the strong arms of their tormentors
in spring under the apple blossoms, saying
     I forgive you, saying: *I can never forgive you,*
saying, *my enemy, my bully, my love.*

First published in *KENYON REVIEW*

JASON SOMMER

INCIDENT AT THE MOTHER'S

It would have been the last thing his mother said
to them, to him and Em, that miserable
visit, early in their marriage,
the final cutting thing
on their way out to the car,
standing before it—

after a weekend of
the usual swipes, some subtle
belittlement or other to share
between them, though more
at Em than him, he thinks,
but truly he forgets
what it was that had him

lunging at his mother—too quick for him
to be amazed at himself, even—
but he did, his arms around her
back and back of the head,
the way you'd catch someone
who was falling over.

Except he was felling her,
swinging her into a waltzer's dip
and an abrupt halt, a hovering tableau
over the front of the car.
He thought he meant to say,

Just shut the hell up. Enough.
Shut up, but as he finished—

his grip, easing, become
a cradling—what came out of him
as he laid her gently down on the hood
was *Shah, shah, shah,   hush—*
shah, shah, shah,   hush—
something from the beginning of
him, of her and him.

First published in *SOU'WESTER*

PESTICIDE II: LIBERTY

For Deb

Remember how we ran through fields
of Queen Anne's lace, shirtless, our sex
still knotted like tiny fists in our chests,
jeans rolled up to the knees? And how our ankles
were crusted with mud from the creek
where we caught frogs and crawdads,
for sport, and let them go? Remember
eating ground cherries and wild raspberries,
sucking the sweet from red clover?
And the clouds of Yellow Sulfur wings
rising around us on days after rain
when they gathered on the drying puddles
in the road? And the neighbor's farm
where we raced through the halls of corn,
risking being sliced by the menacing
green knives, stealing when we were hungry,
tearing an ear open and plunging our teeth
into the firm inviting flesh? The dirt mixed
with sweat. Remember when we thought
what we should fear was the bull
we outran, and the nettles and the ticks? Before
our bodies betrayed us. Before we knew
we were doomed all along. Before we learned
of the real poisons lurking all around us.

Before I started having nightmares,
and you started carrying a gun.

*(This poem is one from a group of poems which take as their titles the
names of registered pesticides.)*

First published in *MIDWESTERN GOTHIC*

_____

WHY AM I NOT INVITED TO YOUR PARTY?

And what are your parties like without me?

Dancing? Is there dancing?

I used to dance. I danced like someone being stung

by ferocious bees. Agony was my means. I danced

to words I've never said aloud:

like scullery and larder.

And whenever what was playing stopped

I poured myself back into my body

like a deer at the side of a highway turning

away from the impulse to cross.

And exactly because I was all over the grid

someone left the party

saddled in the biggest gleaming body, hooved.

So if you keep me off your party list

I guess I can't make myself understand.

More than once I sacrificed my dignity

on the slab of a kitchen island.

More than once I danced off the cliff

and let everyone, first, jump from my back.

It was what we call wonderful, wasn't it?

It was. That's what it was.

First published in *FIELD: CONTEMPORARY POETRY & POETICS*

ANGELA VORAS-HILLS

WATCHING NATURE ON PBS

The caribou calf is separated from the herd, pursued
by the wolf. Unless it slips up, the calf could escape,
outrun it. The toddler grows restless and runs to the window,
watching the garbage truck back up, lift bins, and dump
our trash into itself. I don't redirect her. My own childhood
window looked into a tree. All year, there were branches. Sometimes
covered in leaves, but by winter, they were bare. I often prayed
for a way out. I once spoke directly to God, said: "God, if you know
everything,
what am I thinking now?" And I tried to think the opposite of anything
he'd expect me to think. Another time I said, "God, if you help me
leave this place," but could think of nothing worth giving in return.
No matter how much we bargained, I never asked God to save our house
from fire, even after a house on our block burned down. I didn't
ask him to spare us from cancer, Alzheimer's, any other death. I believed
there was a reason for everything. When my mother asked me
to blow into her cup of dice for luck before she rolled them onto the bar,
I didn't wonder what it meant if she didn't win. Then, in high school,
a classmate was found dead in her bed. Her mother had gone to wake her,
but her heart had stopped beating. The parenting books say it's good
to establish rituals. I run a bath, wash peanut butter from the toddler's hair.
I rock her, sing folk songs about birds, and she sits up, pointing to a spider
climbing the wall. I watch it as I lay her in the crib, still singing
as her eyes close. I wait until she falls asleep.

First published in *NEW OHIO REVIEW*

MARK WAGENAAR

———

A BRIEF REPORT ON COSMOLOGY, FATE & HUMAN FRAILTY

In other news a man walked through the mile of land mines that
    separates the Koreas.
Write this down, a soldier is quoted as saying, as a miracle.

Write it down next to the baby who weighs less than 400 grams, who
    survived the cull
in England because a tiny pair of scissors pushed the scale past the cutoff
    weight.

In other news Ryan has spent three months trying to figure out the
    semiotics
behind his accident, doing 130 in his '91 5.0: Ryan on Ryan Road,
    zooming past

Ryan Ranch, ejected through the sun roof when the car slammed into a
    tree.
He says he cleared the power lines, if you believe it, says none of the
    flashlight-bearers

could find him at first. My life is the encore to a human cannonball act,
    he says,
but I don't how to believe in my life if I can hardly believe the story.

In other news my father quits smoking & never sleeps a full night again.
My mother has a hysterectomy, & never sleeps a full night again,

cycles through Ambien & chamomile, passionflower & melatonin,
      trytophan
& Bud Light, paces the rooms in the hours after midnight the way her
      mother did.

In other news a doctor injects my grandfather with a radioactive dye.
      Brings up the heart
on the screen: the dye coils & twists on the shuddering sea like fishing
      lines gone slack.

The screen is a time machine: my DNA, my heart, my capillaries in fifty
      years, if I'm good
or lucky, the screen is one fate. And beside him I walk out the door into
      the world

of the moth hour, when the honeysuckle opens to the world, to the
      smallest
of tongues, the hour when everything given to us in the hangman's hour
      is taken

piece by piece, each jot & iota, & replaced with silhouettes & cinders, an
      arachnid
moon low on the eastern horizon, angry for the dark threads it left behind

in my grandfather, clouds half-smudged across it, as translucent as the
      tape that will shut
his eyelids on the steel table. The fact that he's going home is another
      entry in this book

the soldier had mentioned, the Book of Little Miracles, with three of four
      valves shut.
There must be a character in that book for the dark behind the characters,
      the same dark

behind the stars. First thing listed is the existence of our universe, the
    second
is our making. It kills me that no one will ever read it. That you cannot
    speak the language

when you tell someone a language is extinct. I hope the wind is just right
    this hour,
that all of the balloons with winter socks tied to them will drift across the
    border

into North Korea, a balloon race of winter socks, a balloon race for all of
    the naked feet
in the winter cold, thousands of globes, too many for the guns, too small
    for the guns.

I hope the triple bypass gives him another day. Here, trace again the
    trajectories of our lives.
Spider, pull your thread. Father, Mother, reel back your dreams. The dead
    are annealed,

buried the way a blacksmith buries a hot blade in sand. And everything
    is a spark,
body & petal & waterdrop, struck sparks, we are struck against the flint of
    our frailty,

we are flashes in the spark plugs, the world an engine in a black car
    Heaven rides to the edge.

First published in *NORTH AMERICAN REVIEW*

D

D is for dragon and damsel, diamond and diadem. For deciduous woods, their dropping leaves. For dew and the dewclaws of deer. For deciduous teeth, delicate as dimes or decimals. For daughters and daughter cells. For Daedalus, who (although dexterous, deliberate, dagger-eyed) could not dam his son's daring. For the dazzling daydream of sun on deep water. For how dizzy the drop. For daughter. D is for danger in daylight or damson dusk. D is for the deportation of other people's daughters under drape of darkness. For Daphne and her despair. For becoming forest and for deforestation. For dales and dells full of delphiniums, for their deflowering. For disenchantment. For how daughters disappear and some are found and some are not. For desert, ditch, and dirt; for dogs and dental records. D is for detonation, damage, decibel. For Demeter and desolation and the way December daubs its dullness on the wall. For the way death comes to some doors dressed as a long-gone daughter. D for the dress you press yourself against.

First published in *FAIRY TALE REVIEW*

RON WALLACE

LOST SOFTNESS SOFTLY MAKES A TRAP FOR US

When we think of all the things in our lives we've lost—
Persons, places, things, and the all the softness
That went with them—and we want, oh so softly,
To call them back from the hole such loss makes

Even memory, time's antagonist, cannot provide a
Hook, a lure, a snare, a tender trap
To keep them in, when all they want is for
Us to let them go, until there is no us.

First published in *THE GOLDEN SHOVEL ANTHOLOGY*

WHEN THE DEVIL LEADS US HOME AND YELLS SURPRISE

Is that your house he asks
This used to be my house I said

But those are not your people
So that can't be your house

But it is my house I said
I had some people maybe a few

Even though those are not your people
Even though they don't look like you

I had to live somewhere I said
This is the house where I lived

But where are your people he said

My people live in a different house
They don't care to know about me

If you're the devil
Why are you asking me questions

The devil said since the house
You had to live in is gone
I thought you'd be happy

It sure is a hot day I said

Of course it is said the devil

Why do you think I work in town

First published in *POETRY*

DYLAN WEIR

———

I'M _____ AND I'M AN ALCOHOLIC

So I've seen my share of corn mash mixed to quicksand.
Felt it spread the swan's neck opposed direction.
Let the metal arm drop into the deep end. I wept
from wash still to base wine to dense vapor. Spent shell
casings like a cicada. Split hell–a splintered cask–
trapping acoustics. Cool it down, distilled to thimbles,
singing milkblood.
I dragged a rake across the moon–my mother's stomach.
They told me once I was a child–I don't believe it.
They said: find the high watermark–dive in headfirst–
had my horse haul loads of rotgut in place of grain.
Me and the teetotalers played tag
to pick who would go to church and who to chalk dust.
Liquid hunches, drinking sacrament,
I feel closer to dead relatives than to my abstinence.
Measured absence in the sickled lips of flasks.
It came natural: licking the plate clean, asking for more.
I am the undrunk son of a son who would run
from an uncle's fists–He is much taller than me,
but we have the same feet. Before grandpa died,
fifty years dry, I asked about his bad brothers and he corrected me:
bad chemicals.
I knew all of this before I stopped drinking
out of sippy cups. My liver's fine
though I am less certain survival is,
itself, so deserving of a song.

First published in *PASSAGES NORTH*

164

MARCUS WICKER

PRAYER ON THE SUBDIVISION

Then I graduate to a four-digit mortgage inside an ornate
      gate. Me
& two more mes: patent attorney & career soldier. A trinity of clean-
ass SUVs parked beside matching beige tri-levels—proof we own
at least 1/3 the Dream, though my Range is only leased. The tender
kin who invented that adage about good fences must have been black
& living in a cul-de-sac trying to mend an unbreachable wall, black

as light stoking an infrared grill—visible as me
& my family braising grass-fed ribs in Guinness until tender
enough to heal an ulcer. Now, that's clean—
Anyway, last spring I host an open house for my niece, figuring I own
the deed, so I can play Frankie Beverly's treatise on loving his own

way loud as I damn well please. Folk slow dancing on a black-
top patio. Auntie Becky louder than the lot of us. D finally clean.
These few, far-between carrots that keep us trotting. The other mes
are curiously unseen despite formal invites & my knocking, tender

as a Girl Scout cookie vendor. & I get it. This tinder
situation, guilt by association at the homeowners'
meeting where I am cited, promptly. Me & only me.
Never mind the Weinsteins' catered blowout where the black
guy gets a knock for weed from their coy teen with the powder-clean

philtrum at an unholy hour. Father, please. Let me stunt, clean
as a Gillette jawline on a solo hunting trip. I'll be a kind of tender-

skinned privilege. A four-sided mirror. Be my own
constitution if living well pleases you. I'd sell my vacation, black-
market-style, for tithe money even. But, please. Don't make me

do it all in Carlton Banks argyle. I don't want to be a clean-
cut member of any club where I can't rock linen loose enough to
let my junk breathe. Because, after all, Father, you made me.

First published in NARRATIVE

JAMEKA WILLIAMS

PLASTIC WHITE GIRL

White guys online want me savage,
draped in beads. Long black nipples,
nothing else.

:

Do not hold me to the light.
I have a lot of browning thorns.

:

Skinned & kinked.
Sally Hemings in leggings.

:

In *Pinky*, Pinky Johnson passes for White.
& still her skin - blue vein surface -
thin enough to witness the yellow in her.

:

Nina Simone's skin was black & slick
with gin sweats. A furious drunk, she never
got a pair of blue eyes for Christmas.

:

Don't leave me, my love.
Tangle your fingers here:
dark roots meets alabaster skull.
(deletes Tinder account)

:

I received a bar of Ivory soap &
a washcloth for Christmas one year.
A plastic white girl the next.

:

Gin is also white.
Simone's teeth: white.

:

I'm drunk: the white walls vibrate
like mice.

:

Simone sang of four women: My name is Aunt Sarah!
Sarah's skin: yellow, her father: rich-white, her black mother:
forced.

:

My Sarahs are foamy leaves rippling through a latte.
My Sarahs get DNA test for birthdays to see if they
have a little Wakanda in them, on their mama's side.

:

Spoiler alert: Pinky puts the wrong skin back on.

First published in *JET FUEL REVIEW*

HOMECOMING

Goddamn the vacuum of a Midwest
winter, when even those hard winds
cannot tremble the withered wheat.
Goddamn the what's-left-to-say dry
& empty in our mouths after eulogy
turns too truthful. Rifle volleys that
shake out the last few hardy birds,
convince me. Drape me like a flag.
Shape me like a coffin. Imagine him
over there; burning sand, hard light.
Believe me the why. Goddamn the
x-rayed December trees, the bullet
still lodged in the skull of night, this
shovel-breaking earth we break &
drape in stars, stripes. Partisan hush
fat between us. Thank you, mother;
goddamn the rest. Let's call a body
a body & never by its name.

First published in *NINTH LETTER*

_____

ON VISITING THE FRANKLIN PARK CONSERVATORY
& BOTANICAL GARDENS

I have come to collect the various species of America:
   ruby-spotted, tigers, kites & pipevines—an armory
of wings & two-week bodies. The room swells openly
   & I ascend to the top—

         I am separate from the boy
            who swats persistently.

Tucked in the corner of a window, a white morpho,
   the only kind to perch long enough for me to satisfy
my collecting—its lunar afterglow still hanging
   as I pulse & pace to get a closer look.

I am separate from the boy who climbs a nearby tower
   & shouts for his father.

Perhaps I am half of this—a set of dots for eyes,
   spine for spine, my insides half my father's—
half my mother's. *Kuv tus ntsuj plig* unlike the fate
   of quick bodies, sovereign cavities, mother
whose torso fell early in harvest—a bed of muscle
   to hold her from splitting in two—

                        & do we hear it?

As in a fever the boy runs back & does not see
    the white morpho the way I must see it:
my personal moon stone-ripe in this foreign corner,
    mother as fauna forever—inhuman & gazing.

Then my body a chariot pulled by a pair of orange helicons
    sweeping towards the main water feature (complete with koi).

This place in which I dream the new body—whole & abiding—

    I am reaching for the boy now as warden to both the living
& the afterliving—the privilege in every gesture—like mother's
    first gifts: name & citizenship, poetry always in departure,
the song about the moon falling over, fast in flames—

First published in POETRY

CONTRIBUTOR BIOGRAPHIES

Lisa Ampleman is the author of two books of poetry, *Romances* (LSU Press, 2020) and *Full Cry* (NFSPS Press, 2013), and a chapbook, *I've Been Collecting This to Tell You* (Kent State UP, 2012). Her poems have appeared in journals such as *Poetry, Image, Kenyon Review Online, 32 Poems, Poetry Daily,* and *Verse Daily.* She lives in Cincinnati, where she is the managing editor of *The Cincinnati Review.*

Geoff Anderson curated the first poetry shows for biracial writers in Columbus, Ohio (The Other Box), translation (Lingua Franca), and immigration (New World). He's a Callaloo fellow and his chapbook, *Humming Dirge*s, won Paper Nautilus's Debut Series (2017). He is assistant poetry editor with *Flypaper Mag,* and he has work in or forthcoming in The *Normal School Online, RHINO, Southern Indiana Review*, and at www.andersongeoff.com.

Derrick Austin is the author of *Trouble the Water* (BOA Editions). A Cave Canem fellow, his work has appeared or is forthcoming in *Best American Poetry, Image: A Journal of Arts and Religion, New England Review, The Nation,* and *Tin House.* He was a finalist for the 2017 Kate Tufts Discovery Award. He is currently a Stegner Fellow in Poetry at Stanford University.

Jeffrey Bean is Professor of English/Creative Writing at Central Michigan University. He is author of two chapbooks and the poetry collections *Diminished Fifth* (WordTech) and *Woman Putting on Pearl*s (Red Mountain Press), winner of the 2016 Red Mountain Prize for Poetry. His poems have been featured on *The Writer's Almanac*, in the 2014 and 2016 *New Poetry from the Midwest* anthologies, and in the anthology *Good Poems, American Places.* Recent poems appear or are forthcoming in *The Southern Review, Verse Daily, Poets.Org, The Antioch Review, The Missouri Review*, and *Willow Springs*, among other journals. Find him online at www.jeffreybeanpoet.com.

Joy Belonger is a queer transfeminine writer, educator, and printmaker from Chicago, Illinois. They hold an MFA from the Iowa Writers' Workshop, where they were an instructor and writing fellow. Previous work has appeared in *Barrelhouse, Black Warrior Review, Cleaver, Nat. Brut, TIMBER*, and elsewhere.

Bryce Berkowitz is the author of *Bermuda Ferris Wheel,* winner of the 42 Miles Press Poetry Award (forthcoming 2020). His writing has appeared or is forthcoming in *Best New Poets, The Sewanee Review, Ninth Letter, Nashville Review, the minnesota review, Salt Hill,* and other publications. He teaches at Butler University.

Kimberly Blaeser is the author of three poetry collections—most recently *Apprenticed to Justice*; and the editor of *Traces in Blood, Bone, and Stone: Contemporary Ojibwe Poetry.* She served as Wisconsin Poet Laureate for 2015-2016. Her scholarship, creative nonfiction, fiction, and poetry have been widely anthologized. A Professor of English and Native American Studies at the University of Wisconsin-Milwaukee, Blaeser is also on faculty for the Institute of American Indian Arts low rez MFA program in Santa Fe. Blaeser is Anishinaabe, an enrolled member of the Minnesota Chippewa Tribe, and grew up on White Earth Reservation. A fourth collection of poetry, *Copper Yearning*, will be released from Holy Cow! Press in fall 2019.

Traci Brimhall is the author of three collections of poetry, most recently *Saudade* (Copper Canyon Press, 2017). She works as an Assistant Professor of Creative Writing at Kansas State University.

Mary M. Brown lives with her husband Bill in Anderson, Indiana. Retired now, she taught literature and creative writing at Indiana Wesleyan for many years and was an editor of *The Steinbeck Review.* Her work appears on the *Poetry Foundation* and *American Life in Poetry* websites and recently in *Third Wednesday, Flying Island, Plough,* and *JJournal.*

Anders Carlson-Wee is the author of *The Low Passions* (W.W. Norton, 2019). His work has appeared in *BuzzFeed, Ploughshares, Virginia Quarterly Review, New England Review, Poetry Daily, The Sun, Best New Poets, The Best American Nonrequired Reading,* and many other places. The recipient of fellowships from the National Endowment for the Arts, the McKnight Foundation, the Camargo Foundation, Bread Loaf, Sewanee, and the Napa Valley Writers' Conference, he is the winner of Ninth Letter's Poetry Award as well as the 2017 Poetry International Prize. His work has been translated into Chinese. Anders holds an MFA from Vanderbilt University and lives in Minneapolis. Find him online at www.anderscarlsonwee.com.

Sarah Carson is the author of the poetry collections *Poems in Which You Die* and *Buick City.* Her poetry and other writing have appeared in *DIAGRAM, Guernica, the minnesota review, the Nashville Review,* and *New Ohio Review,* among others. She has been the recipient of a grant from the Illinois Arts Council and finalist for the Ruth Lilly and Dorothy Sargent Rosenberg fellowship from the Poetry Foundation. She lives in Michigan with her daughter and two dogs.

Robin Chapman is author of ten books of poetry, most recently *The Only Home We Know* (Tebot Bach, 2019). She is a recipient of Appalachia's 2010 Helen Howe Poetry Prize, the Wisconsin Library Association Prize for Outstanding Achievement in Book of Poetry (2008, 2017), and the Posner Poetry Award (1999, 2005), and the Cider Press Review Editors' Prize. Her poems have appeared recently in *Alaska Quarterly Review, Prairie Schooner,* and *Valparaiso Poetry Review.*

Leila Chatti is a Tunisian American poet. She earned an MFA in poetry from North Carolina State University, where she was awarded the Academy of American Poets Prize. She is the recipient of grants from the Barbara Deming Memorial Fund and the Helene Wurlitzer Foundation of New Mexico, and fellowships and scholarships from the Fine Arts Work Center in Provincetown, the Wisconsin Institute for Creative Writing, the Tin House Writers' Workshop, The Frost Place Conference on Poetry, the Key West Literary Seminars, and Dickinson House. Her poems have received prizes from Ploughshares' Emerging Writer's Contest, Narrative's 30 Below Contest, and the Gregory O'Donoghue International Poetry Prize, among others, and appear in *Best New Poets* (2015 & 2017), *Ploughshares, Tin House, American Poetry Review, Virginia Quarterly Review, The Georgia Review, New England Review, Kenyon Review Online, Narrative, The Rumpus,* and other journals and anthologies. In 2017, she was shortlisted for the Brunel International African Poetry Prize. She currently serves as the Consulting Poetry Editor at *The Raleigh Review* and lives in Cleveland, Ohio, where she is the inaugural Anisfield-Wolf Fellow in Writing and Publishing at Cleveland State University.

Suman Chhabra is a multigenre writer. She holds a B.A. from the University of Michigan and an MFA in Writing from the School of the Art Institute of Chicago. Chhabra is the author of *Demons Off,* a chapbook through Meekling Press. She is a Kundiman Fellow and Midwest regional chair. Her work has been supported by The Poetry Foundation, Vermont Studio Center, Ragdale, *The Massachusetts Review, TAYO,* and *Homonym* among others. Chhabra teaches courses in Reading and Writing at the School of the Art Institute of Chicago.

Paula Cisewski's fourth poetry collection, *Quitter,* won the Diode Editions Book Prize. She is also the author of *The Threatened Everything* (Burnside Review Books), *Ghost Fargo* (Nightboat Poetry Prize winner, selected by Franz Wright), *Upon Arrival* (Black Ocean), and several chapbooks, including the lyric prose *Misplaced Sinister.* She lives in Minneapolis, where she teaches, collaborates with fellow artists and activists, and serves on the editorial staff of Conduit.

Christopher Citro is the author of *If We Had a Lemon We'd Throw It and Call That the Sun* (Elixir Press, 2020), winner of the 2019 Antivenom Poetry Award, and *The Maintenance of the Shimmy-Shammy* (Steel Toe Books, 2015). His awards include a 2019 fellowship from Ragdale

Foundation and a 2018 Pushcart Prize for Poetry. Recent poetry appears in *Ploughshares, Crazyhorse, The Missouri Review, Gulf Coast, Best New Poets, Pleiades, Narrative, Blackbird,* and *Alaska Quarterly Review.* His creative nonfiction appears in *Boulevard, Quarterly West, The Florida Review, Passages North,* and *Colorado Review.* He teaches creative writing at SUNY Oswego and lives in Syracuse, New York.

George David Clark is an assistant professor of English and creative writing at Washington & Jefferson College. His first book, *Reveille* (Arkansas, 2015), won the Miller Williams Prize, and his recent poems can be found in *AGNI, The Georgia Review, The Gettysburg Review, Image, Ninth Letter, The Southern Review,* and elsewhere. The editor of *32 Poems,* he lives with his wife and their four young children in Washington, Pennsylvania.

Tiana Clark is the author of the poetry collection, *I Can't Talk About the Trees Without the Blood* (University of Pittsburgh Press, 2018), winner of the 2017 Agnes Lynch Starrett Prize, and *Equilibrium* (Bull City Press, 2016), selected by Afaa Michael Weaver for the 2016 Frost Place Chapbook Competition. Clark is a 2019 National Endowment for the Arts Literature Fellow and a recipient of a 2019 Pushcart Prize, as well as a winner of the 2017 Furious Flower's Gwendolyn Brooks Centennial Poetry Prize and 2015 Rattle Poetry Prize. She was the 2017-2018 Jay C. and Ruth Halls Poetry Fellow at the Wisconsin Institute of Creative Writing. Clark is the recipient of scholarships and fellowships to the Bread Loaf Writers' Conference, Sewanee Writers' Conference, and Kenyon Review Writers Workshop. She is a graduate of Vanderbilt University (M.F.A) and Tennessee State University (B.A.) where she studied Africana and Women's studies. Her writing has appeared in or is forthcoming from *The New Yorker, Poetry Magazine, VQR, Tin House Online, Kenyon Review, BuzzFeed News, American Poetry Review, New England Review, Oxford American, Best New Poets 2015,* and elsewhere. She teaches creative writing at Southern Illinois University at Edwardsville.

Andrew Collard lives in Kalamazoo, MI, where he attends grad school and teaches. His poems can be found in *Ploughshares, Mid-American Review,* and *Sixth Finch,* among other journals.

J.L. Conrad is the author of the full-length collection *A Cartography of Birds* (Louisiana State University Press) and the chapbook *NOT IF BUT WHEN,* which won Salt Hill's third annual Dead Lake Chapbook Competition. Her poems have appeared in *Pleiades, Jellyfish, Salamander, The Beloit Poetry Journal, H_NGM_N, The Laurel Review* and *Forklift, Ohio,* among others. She lives in Madison, Wisconsin.

Born and raised in the Midwest, **Caitlin Cowan's** poetry, fiction, and nonfiction have appeared in *THRUSH Poetry Journal, New Ohio Review, Pleiades, SmokeLong Quarterly, Rappahannock Review,* and elsewhere. A finalist for the Levis Prize in Poetry and a semifinalist for the Boston Discovery Poetry Contest, she has won the Littoral Press Poetry Prize, the Mississippi Review Prize, the Ron McFarland Prize for Poetry, and an Avery Hopwood Award. She holds a PhD in English and has taught writing at the University of North Texas, Texas Woman's University, and Interlochen Center for the Arts. She works, travels, and teaches for Blue Lake Fine Arts Camp in Twin Lake, Michigan. Find her at caitlincowan.com.

Brian Czyzyk is an MFA candidate in poetry at Purdue University. Originally from northern Michigan, he has work published and forthcoming in *Midwestern Gothic, Nimrod, Colorado Review,* and elsewhere. He wishes you the best.

Alexandria Delcourt received her MFA from the Stonecoast MFA in Creative Writing Program in 2014. She is currently a Lecturer in the Languages & Literatures Department at the University of Wisconsin-Whitewater where she teaches Creative Writing, English, and Race and Ethnic Studies. Her work has appeared in *Written River, Cream City Review, PROFANE, Split Rock, Poetry Quarterly, As/Us: A Space for*

Women of the World, Kalyani Magazine, FULCRUM: An Annual of Poetry and Aesthetics, Aster(ix), and other publications. She lives in Madison, Wisconsin.

Darren C. Demaree is the author of fourteen poetry collections, most recently *"Unfinished Murder Ballads", (October 2020, Backlash Press).* He is the recipient of a 2018 Ohio Arts Council Individual Excellence Award, the Louis Bogan Award from Trio House Press, and the Nancy Dew Taylor Award from *Emrys Journal.* He is the Managing Editor of the *Best of the Net Anthology* and *Ovenbird Poetry.* He lives in Columbus, Ohio, with his wife and children.

Heather Derr-Smith is a poet with four books, *Each End of the World* (Main Street Rag Press, 2005), *The Bride Minaret* (University of Akron Press, 2008), *Tongue Screw* (Spark Wheel Press, 2016), and *Thrust* (Persea Books, 2017), which won the Lexi Rudnitsky/Editor's Choice Award. Her work has appeared in *Fence, Crazyhorse,* and *Missouri Review.* She is managing director of Cuvaj Se, a nonprofit that supports writers in conflict zones and post-conflict zones, and divides her time mostly between Des Moines, Iowa, where she lives with her family and Sarajevo, Bosnia, where she teaches poetry workshops with survivors of trauma.

Joanne Diaz is the recipient of fellowships from the Illinois Arts Council, the National Endowment for the Arts, and the Sustainable Arts Foundation. She is the author of *My Favorite Tyrants* (University of Wisconsin Press, 2014) and *The Lessons* (Silverfish Review Press, 2011), and with Ian Morris, she is the co-editor of *The Little Magazine in Contemporary America* (University of Chicago Press, 2015). She is an Associate Professor of English at Illinois Wesleyan University.

Nicole M. K. Eiden is an award-winning poet and filmmaker interested in exploring the common challenges and beauty of ordinary life. She arrived in New Orleans in 1999 from Columbus, Ohio, and, though she has never looked to go back, she does often look back. She won third place in the 2016 Women's National Book Association writing contest for "Mortgage," a poem from her debut collection, *I Am One of You* (Mississippi Sound, 2016). She holds a Master of Fine Arts degree from the University of New Orleans and a Bachelor of Communications degree in video production from Ohio University. Additionally, Nicole co-owns Windowsill Pies, a Southern-style pie and tart company in New Orleans, where she lives with her husband and daughter.

An Illinois native, **Matthew Fash** holds a BA in English from Indiana State University. Their work has been published in *Allusions, Open: Journal of Arts and Letters,* and *Raw Art Review.* They believe very much in the power of creeks and cornfields.

Jeremy Flick holds a Master's Degree in Creative Writing from Ball State University and an MFA from University of Kentucky. His poetry has been published in *The Matador Review, The Broken Plate, Pidgeonholes*, and others. His book reviews have appeared in *The Hollins Critic* and *Rain Taxi*. His website is: jeremyaflick.com

Rebecca Morgan Frank is the author of *Sometimes We're All Living in a Foreign Country* (Carnegie Mellon UP, 2017), *The Spokes of Venus* (Carnegie Mellon UP, 2016), and *Little Murders Everywhere*, a finalist for the Kate Tufts Discovery Award. Her poems have appeared such places at *The New Yorker, American Poetry Review,* and *Ploughshares*, and she is the recipient of the Poetry Society of America's Alice Fay di Castagnola Award for her manuscript-in-progress. Cofounder and editor-in-chief of the online magazine *Memorious*, she is currently the Distinguished Visiting Writer at Bowling Green State University and resides in Oak Park, Illinois.

Molly Fuller is is the author of the prose poetry collection, *For Girls Forged by Lightning: Prose & Other Poems* (All Nations Press), which was selected for *The Wardrobe*'s "Best Dressed" feature (Sundress Publications). Her chapbooks are *The Neighborhood Psycho Dreams*

of Love (Cutty Wren Press) and *Tender the Body* (Spare Change Press); her sequence "Hold Your Breath" was included in *Nothing to Declare: A Guide to the Flash Sequence* (Marie Alexander/White Pine Press). Fuller's prose poems and micro fictions have appeared in journals and anthologies including *100 Word Story, Blue Earth Review, Dressing Room Poetry Journal, Hot Metal Bridge, Kestrel, MadHatLit, NANO Fiction, The Oklahoma Review,* and *The Potomac.* She was a semifinalist for The *Florida Review's* Jeanne Leiby Memorial Chapbook Award and a finalist for the Key West Literary Seminar's Emerging Writer Award. She received her MFA from Sarah Lawrence College and is currently the Director of the International Raymond Carver Society. She lives in Ohio.

Max Garland is the author of *Postal Confessions, Hunger Wide as Heaven,* and *The Word We Used for It,* winner of the 2017-18 Brittingham Prize. Garland is Professor Emeritus at the University of Wisconsin-Eau Claire, former Wisconsin Poet Laureate, and a writer-in-residence for the city of Eau Claire.

Adam J. Gellings is a poet and instructor from Columbus, Ohio. His previous work has appeared in *Best New Poets 2017, Prelude,* and *Salamander.*

Jason Gray is the author of *Radiation King,* winner of the Idaho Prize for Poetry, and *Photographing Eden,* as well as two chapbooks, *How to Paint the Savior Dead* and *Adam & Eve Go to the Zoo.* His poems have been featured in *Poetry, Kenyon Review, American Poetry Review, Image,* and elsewhere.

Gail Griffin is the author of four works of nonfiction, including *"The Events of October": Murder-Suicide on a Small Campus* (2010) and the forthcoming *Grief's Country: A Memoir in Pieces* (Wayne State U. Press, 2020). She is the winner of *New Ohio Review's* Nonfiction Prize as well as poetry prizes at *Calyx* and *Folio.* Seven poems from her poetry chapbook, *Virginals,* were featured in *The Missouri Review.* Her poetry, essays, and brief nonfiction have appeared in other journals such as *Fourth Genre, Solstice,* and *Chattahoochie Review,* and anthologies including *Fresh Water: Women Writing on the Great Lakes.*

Susan Grimm is a two-time recipient of the Ohio Arts Council Individual Artist Grant. Her poems have been published in *Poetry East, The Cincinnati Review, The Journal,* and *Blackbird.* Her chapbook *Almost Home* was published in 1997. In 2004, BkMk Press published *Lake Erie Blue,* a full-length poetry collection. In 2010, Grimm won the inaugural Copper Nickel Poetry Prize. In 2011, she won the Hayden Carruth Poetry Prize and her chapbook *Roughed Up by the Sun's Mothering Tongue* was published. Visit her blog, The White Space Inside the Poem: http://thewhitespaceinsidethepoem.blogspot.com.

Nicholas Gulig is a Thai-American poet from Wisconsin. He is the first-place winner of the Wisconsin People & Ideas 2017 Poetry Contest. Educated in Montana, Iowa, and Colorado, Gulig earned a Fulbright Fellowship to Bangkok, Thailand, in 2011. His published works include the book-length poems *North of Order* and *Book of Lake.* He lives in Fort Atkinson and teaches at the University of Wisconsin-Whitewater.

Roy G. Guzmán is a Honduran poet whose first collection is coming out from Graywolf Press in 2020. Raised in Miami, Florida, Roy is the recipient of a 2019 grant from the National Endowment for the Arts. In 2017, they were named a Ruth Lilly and Dorothy Sargent Rosenberg Poetry Fellow. They are also the recipient of a 2017 Minnesota State Arts Board Initiative grant and the 2016 Gesell Award for Excellence in Poetry. Their work has been included in the *Best New Poets 2017* anthology, guest-edited by Natalie Diaz, and *Best of the Net 2017,* guest-edited by Eduardo C. Corral. Roy holds degrees from the University of Minnesota, Dartmouth College, the University of Chicago, and the Honors College at Miami Dade College. They currently live in Minneapolis, where they are pursuing a PhD in Cultural Studies (Comparative Studies in Discourse and Society) at the University of Minnesota.

Rebecca Hazelton is the author of the New York Times New and Noteworthy book of poetry *Gloss*, as well as *Fair Copy* (Ohio State University Press, 2012), winner of the 2011 Ohio State University Press / The Journal Award in Poetry, and *Vow* (Cleveland State University Press, 2013). She was the 2010-11 Jay C. and Ruth Halls Poetry Fellow at the University of Wisconsin, Madison Creative Writing Institute and winner of the "Discovery" / Boston Review 2012 Poetry Contest. A two time Pushcart prize winner, her poems have appeared in *Poetry, The New Yorker, Best American Poetry* (2013, 2015), and *The New Yorker.*

Geramee Hensley is a writer living in Ohio. He wants to know about hunger. His work has been featured or is forthcoming in *Button Poetry, Indiana Review, The Shallow Ends, The Margins, The Recluse*, and others. You can find him on geramee.com, where he curates the Bleeding Hearts Club, a new digital community centered around exploring heartbreak in poetry.

Rebekah Denison Hewitt holds an MFA from the University of Wisconsin-Madison where she was the Martha Meier Renk Graduate Fellow. She is an associate poetry editor at Orison Books, and her work has appeared in *Gulf Stream, The Pinch, Narrative Magazine,* and *The Rumpus,* among others. She lives in Wisconsin with her husband and children.

Catherine Jagoe is the author or translator of eight books of poetry, fiction, and literary criticism, and a Pushcart Prize winner for her nonfiction. Her poetry book *Bloodroot* was awarded the 2016 Settlement House prize and the Council for Wisconsin Writers' 2016 Poetry Book Award. Born in the U.K., she now makes her home in Madison, Wisconsin.

Marlin M. Jenkins was born and raised in Detroit and is the author of the poetry chapbook *Capable Monsters* (Bull City Press, 2020). His poetry and fiction have been given homes by *Indiana Review, The Rumpus, Waxwing,* and *The Iowa Review,* among others. He earned his MFA in poetry at the

University of Michigan and currently lives in Saint Paul, Minnesota. You can find him online at marlinmjenkins.com.

Mark Kraushaar's poetry has been included in Best American Poetry, Ploughshares, and Yale Review was well as the website Poetry Daily and Ted Kooser's American Life in Poetry. He has been a recipient of Poetry Northwest's Richard Hugo Award. A full length collection, Falling Brick Kills Local Man, was published by University of Wisconsin Press and awarded the 2009 Felix Pollak Prize. A recent collection, The Uncertainty Principle, published by Waywiser Press, was chosen by James Fenton as winner of the Anthony Hecht Prize you. Mark has worked as a pipe welder, wig salesman, shoe factory line worker, waiter, motel clerk, and most recently as an RN.

C. Kubasta writes poetry, prose and hybrid forms. She is the author of several poetry books, most recently *Of Covenants* (Whitepoint, 2017). Her fiction includes *Girling* (Brain Mill, 2017) and *This Business of the Flesh* (Apprentice House, 2018). She is active with the Wisconsin Fellowship of Poets, and serves as Assistant Poetry Editor with Brain Mill Press. Find her at www.ckubasta.com and follow her @CKubastathePoet.

Josh Lefkowitz was born and raised in the suburbs of Detroit. He attended the University of Michigan where he received the Avery Hopwood Award for Poetry. His poems and essays have been published in *The New York Times, Washington Square Review, Painted Bride Quarterly, Electric Literature, The Millions, The Rumpus, Barrelhouse online, Contrary, Conduit, Shooter Literary Magazine* (UK), *Southword Journal* (Ireland), *Broadview Press* (Canada), and many other places. He has also recorded humor pieces for NPR and the BBC, and his poems have been read aloud on *All Things Considered* and *WNYC*. He has received residencies from the Atlantic Center for the Arts, Berkeley Repertory Theatre, and the New York Mills Regional Cultural Center, Minnesota.

Issa M. Lewis is the author of *Infinite Collisions* (Finishing Line Press, 2017) and a graduate of New England College's MFA program. A runner-up in the 2017 Lois Cranston Memorial Poetry Prize and 2013 winner of the Lucille Clifton Poetry Prize, her poems have appeared in journals such as *Split Rock Review, Pearl,* and *Panoply.*

D.A. Lockhart is the author of seven collections of poetry, including *Devil in the Woods* (Brick Books 2019) and *Tukhone* (Black Moss Press 2020). His work has appeared in *Best Canadian Poetry in English 2019, TriQuarterly, ARC Poetry Magazine, Grain,* Belt, and *the Malahat Review* among many. He is a Turtle Clan member of Eelünaapéewi Lahkéewiit (Lenape), a registered member of the Moravian of the Thames First Nation, and currently resides at the south shore of Waawiiyaatanong (Windsor,ON-Detroit, MI). His work has been generously supported by the Ontario Arts Council and the Canada Council for the Arts. He is the publisher at Urban Farmhouse Press and poetry editor for the Windsor Review.

Kim Lozano was born and raised in Kansas. She now lives in Missouri and teaches creative writing for the St. Louis Writers Workshop and St. Louis Oasis, a lifelong learning organization for people over 50. Her work has been published in *Poetry Daily, The Iowa Review, Alaska Quarterly Review, North American Review, Denver Quarterly, American Life in Poetry* and elsewhere.

Charles Malone grew up in rural Northeastern Ohio, headed west to the Rockies, came back to the Great Lakes, and has loved all of it. Charlie's chapbook *Questions about Circulation* is forthcoming with Driftwood Press as part of the Adrift Chapbook Series. He edited the collection *A Poetic Inventory of Rocky Mountain National Park* with Wolverine Farm Publishing and has work recently published or forthcoming in *Hotel Amerika, The Best of Boneshaker: A Bicycling Almanac, The Sugar House Review, The Dunes Review, Saltfront,* and *Matter: Nomad.* Charlie now works at the Wick Poetry Center at Kent State University coordinating community outreach programs.

Sandra Marchetti is the author of *Confluence*, a full-length collection of poetry from Sundress Publications (2015). She is also the author of four chapbooks of poetry and lyric essays, including *Sight Lines* (Speaking of Marvels Press, 2016), *Heart Radicals* (ELJ Publications, 2015), *A Detail in the Landscape* (Eating Dog Press, 2014), and *The Canopy* (MWC Press, 2012). Sandra's poetry appears widely in *Poet Lore, Blackbird, Ecotone, Southwest Review, River Styx,* and elsewhere. Her essays can be found at *The Rumpus, Whiskey Island, Mid-American Review, Barrelhouse, Pleiades,* and other venues. Sandy earned an MFA in Creative Writing-Poetry from George Mason University and now serves as the Coordinator of Tutoring Services at the College of DuPage in the Chicagoland area.

John McCarthy is the author of *Scared Violent like Horses* (Milkweed Editions, 2019), which was the winner of the 2017 Jake Adam York Prize. He is also the author of *Ghost County* (Midwestern Gothic Press, 2016), which was named a Best Poetry Book of 2016 by The Chicago Review of Books. John is the winner of The Pinch 2016 Literary Award in Poetry, and his work has appeared in *American Literary Review, Best New Poets 2015, Copper Nickel, Hayden's Ferry Review, New Ohio Review, Passages North, Sycamore Review, TriQuarterly, Zone 3*, and in anthologies such as *New Poetry from the Midwest 2017*. He received his MFA from Southern Illinois University Carbondale and currently lives in Evanston, Illinois.

John McCracken is a poet and freelance writer from Madison, Wisconsin, whose work has appeared in *OCCULUM, Drunk in a Midnight Choir, Pressure Gauge Journal,* and the side of a Madison Metro Transit Bus. He is a Staff Reviewer for *Glass: A Journal of Poetry* and provides culture and arts coverage for *Tone Madison*. He is also a member of the board of directors for a local arts and music venue, Communication. He can be found playing drums and yelling in a loud rock band called ghostar.

Michael Mlekoday is a Minnesotan. The author of one collection of poems, *The Dead Eat Everything* (Kent State UP, 2014), Mlekoday holds an MFA from Indiana University and is currently a PhD candidate in English at the University of California, Davis. Their work has appeared or is forthcoming in *Ploughshares, Hayden's Ferry Review, Southern Indiana Review, Washington Square Review,* and other venues.

Simone Muench is the author of six books, including *Wolf Centos* (Sarabande, 2014). Her recent, *Suture*, includes sonnets written with Dean Rader (BLP, 2017). She is an editor of *They Said: A Multi-Genre Anthology of Contemporary Collaborative Writing* (BLP, 2018) and curator of the HB Sunday Reading Series in Chicago. Additionally, she serves as chief faculty advisor for *Jet Fuel Review* and as a senior poetry editor for *Tupelo Quarterly.*

Amy Newman is the author of five books of poetry, most recently *On this Day in Poetry History* (Persea, 2016). She teaches at Northern Illinois University.

Christopher Nelson is the author of *Blood Aria* (University of Wisconsin Press, 2021) and three chapbooks: *Blue House* (Poetry Society of America, 2009), *Capital City at Midnight*, recipient of the 2014 *BLOOM* Chapbook Prize; and *Love Song for the New World* (Seven Kitchens Press, 2019). He is the founder and editor of Green Linden Press and the journal *Under a Warm Green Linden*. Visit christophernelson.info.

Matthew Olzmann was born in Detroit, Michigan. He received a BA from the University of Michigan–Dearborn and an MFA from Warren Wilson College. He is the author of *Contradictions in the Design* (Alice James Books, 2016) and *Mezzanines* (Alice James Books, 2013), winner of the 2011 Kundiman Poetry Prize. Olzmann has received fellowships from the Kresge Arts Foundation and Kundiman, among others. He teaches at Warren Wilson College and lives in North Carolina with his wife, the poet Vievee Francis.

Olatunde Osinaike is a Nigerian-American poet and software developer, originally from the West Side of Chicago. He is the author of the chapbooks *Speech Therapy*, a winner in the Atlas Review's 2019 Chapbook Series, and *The New Knew* (Thirty West). A Best of the Net, Bettering American Poetry, and Pushcart Prize nominee, his work has been selected as winner of the Lucille Clifton Poetry Prize, a winner of the Frontier Industry Prize, honorable mention for the Ploughshares Emerging Writer's Award in Poetry, and as a finalist for the Southeast Review Gearhart Poetry Prize and RHINO Poetry Editor's Prize. His most recent work has appeared, or is forthcoming, in *Best New Poets 2018, Kweli, Glass: A Journal of Poetry, Cosmonauts Avenue, Prelude, Puerto del Sol,* and *Columbia Poetry Review*, among other publications. He has previously served on poetry staff at *The Adroit Journal* and you can find him at www.olatundeosinaike.com.

Hai-Dang Phan is the author of *Reenactments* (Sarabande Books, 2019). His poems have appeared in *The New Yorker, Poetry,* and *Best American Poetry 2016,* and he is the recipient of a National Endowment of the Arts Literature Fellowship. Born in Vietnam and raised in Wisconsin, he holds a Ph.D. in English from the University of Wisconsin-Madison and an M.F.A. in Creative Writing from the University of Florida. Currently, he teaches at Grinnell College and lives in Iowa City.

Kimberly Ann Priest is the author of *Slaughter the One Bird* (Sundress 2021), *Still Life* (PANK 2020), *Parrot Flower* (Glass 2020) and *White Goat Black Sheep* (FLP 2018). An MFA graduate of New England College, she is an assistant professor at Michigan State University, poetry editor for the Nimrod International Journal of Prose and Poetry, and Embody reader for The Maine Review. Her work has appeared in *The Berkeley Poetry Review, The Meadow, Moon City Review*, and *Borderlands*.

Mary Quade grew up in Wisconsin, went to school in Illinois and Iowa, and has lived in Ohio since 2002. She's the author of two poetry collections, *Guide to Native Beasts* (Cleveland State) and *Local Extinctions* (Gold Wake). She teaches creative writing at Hiram College.

Dean Rader's debut collection of poems, *Works & Days*, won the 2010 T. S. Eliot Poetry Prize and Landscape Portrait Figure Form (2014) was named a Best Poetry Book by The Barnes and Noble Review. Three books appeared in 2017: *Self-Portrait as Wikipedia Entry* (Copper Canyon), *Suture*, collaborative poems written with Simone Muench (Black Lawrence Press); and *Bullets into Bells: Poets and Citizens Respond to Gun Violence*, edited with Brian Clements & Alexandra Teague (Beacon). Most recently, he co-edited *They Said: Contemporary Collaborative Writing* and *Native Voices: Poems, Craft, and Conversations*. Dean writes regularly for *The San Francisco Chronicle, The Huffington Post, BOMB*, and *The Kenyon Review*.

Divya Rajan is a Chicago based poet and regulatory scientist. A former poetry editor at *The Furnace Review*, she has published work in *Asian Cha, Rattle, Missouri Review, MAYDAY Magazine, Berfrois, The Missing Slate*, and *After Hours*, as well as the anthologies *New Poetry from the Midwest* and *Silk and Spice*. Her work has been nominated for Pushcart and Best of the Net multiple times. Recently, her poems were translated into Chinese by the good folks at *Voice and Verse* magazine in Hong Kong.

Karen Rigby is the author of *Chinoiserie* (Ahsahta Press, 2012). A 2007 National Endowment for the Arts literature fellow, she has published poems in *jubilat, Bennington Review, The London Magazine, Field* and other journals.

Sarah M. Sala is the author of *Devil's Lake* (Tolsun 2020). Her work appears in *BOMB, Michigan Quarterly Review, The Southampton Review, The Stockholm Review of Literature*, and *Poetry Ireland Review*, among others. The founding director of Office Hours Poetry Workshop, she is assistant poetry editor for *the Bellevue Literary Review*, and teaches expository writing at New York University. www.sarahsala.com

Robin Beth Schaer is the author of the poetry collection *Shipbreaking* (2015), and her poems and essays have appeared in *Tin House, Paris Review*, and *Guernica*, among others. She lives in Ohio with her family and is a Visiting Assistant Professor in Creative Writing at Oberlin College.

Max Schleicher was born in Milwaukee, Wisconsin and has lived around the Great Lakes for much of his life. He is currently is a Phd student at the University of Utah. His poems have appeared in the Mid American Review, Zocalo Public Square, the Manchester Review, and other places. He can be found tweeting about baseball and the Upper Midwest at @ maxschl.

Bruce Snider is the author of the poetry collections, *Fruit* (forthcoming Spring 2020), *Paradise, Indiana, and The Year We Studied Women*. He is co-editor with the poet Shara Lessley of *The Poem's Country: Place and Poetic Practice*. His poems have appeared in T*he American Poetry Review, Best American Poetry 2012, Harvard Review, New England Review, Poetry,* and *Threepenny Review*, among others. He is currently an Associate Professor at the University of San Francisco.

Jason Sommer is the author of five poetry collections: *Portulans* (forthcoming from the University of Chicago Press), *Lifting the Stone* (Forest Books), *Other People's Troubles* (University of Chicago Press), *The Man Who Sleeps in My Office* (University of Chicago Press), and *The Laughter of Adam and Eve* (Southern Illinois University Press), which won the Crab Orchard Review Prize. He has published translations of Irish language poems and collaborative translations of Chinese fiction. Among other awards, he has held a Stegner Fellowship in Poetry from Stanford University and a Whiting Foundation Writer's Fellowship, as well as fellowships from the Sewanee and Bread Loaf writers conferences. Recent work has appeared in *Ploughshares, The Cincinnati Review,* and *Sou'wester* and on the *Poetry Daily* website.

Heather Swan is the author of *A Kinship with Ash* (Terrapin Books, 2020), the chapbook, *The Edge of Damage*, and the nonfiction book, *Where Honeybees Thrive*. Her poems have appeared in *Phoebe, The Raleigh Review, Cold Mountain Review, Midwestern Gothic, About Place,* and

Basalt, among others. Her nonfiction has appeared in *Aeon, ISLE, Belt Magazine, Minding Nature,* and *Edge Effects.* She teaches writing and environmental literature at University of Wisconsin-Madison.

Lee Upton was born in St. Johns, Michigan, and lived until her early twenties in Michigan. She graduated from Michigan State University and often uses her memories of Michigan for settings in her writing. Lee's most recent books are *Visitations: Stories* (LSU Press) and *Bottle the Bottles the Bottles the Bottles: Poem*s (Cleveland State University Poetry Center).

Angela Voras-Hills lives with her family in Milwaukee, Wisconsin. Her first book, *Louder Birds* (Pleiades 2020), received the Lena-Miles Wever Todd Poetry Prize. Individual poems have appeared in K*enyon Review Online, Best New Poets,* and *New Ohio Review,* among other journals and anthologies. She has received grants from The Sustainable Arts Foundation and Key West Literary Seminar, as well as a fellowship at Writers' Room of Boston.

Mark Wagenaar has lived in the Midwest for years, off and on, through a B.A. at Graceland University, an M.A. at the University of Northern Iowa, and now as an assistant professor at Valparaiso University, in Indiana. He is the author of three award-winning poetry collections, including the Saltman Prize-winning *Southern Tongues Leave Us Shining,* just released from Red Hen Press. His fiction and poetry appear widely, including in T*he New Yorker, Tin House, The Southern Review, Gulf Coast, the Cincinnati Review,* and *River Styx,* among many others, and his poems have won a variety of awards, including the James Wright Poetry Award, the Mary C. Mohr Poetry Prize, the CBC Poetry Award, and the *Tupelo Quarterly* Poetry Prize.

Claire Wahmanholm is the author of *Night Vision* (New Michigan Press, 2017), *Wilder* (Milkweed Editions, 2018), and *Redmouth* (Tinderbox Editions, 2019). A 2020 McKnight Writing Fellow, her poems have recently appeared in, or are forthcoming from, *Copper Nickel, Image,*

Great River Review, Beloit Poetry Journal, *Grist, RHINO, The Los Angeles Review, West Branch, Southeast Review*, and *DIAGRAM*, and have been featured on *Verse Daily, Poetry Daily*, and t*he Academy of American Poets Poem-a-Day* series. She lives and teaches in the Twin Cities.

Ron Wallace is Felix Pollak Professor Emeritus at the University of Wisconsin-Madison. His most recent books are *For Dear Life* and F*or a Limited Time Only*, both from the University of Pittsburgh Press. He divides his time between Madison and a forty-acre farm in Bear Valley, Wisconsin.

Nikki Wallschlaeger's work has been featured in *The Nation, Brick, American Poetry Review, Witness, Kenyon Review, POETRY*, and others. She is the author of the full-length collections *Houses* (Horseless Press 2015) and *Crawlspace* (Bloof 2017) as well as the graphic book *I Hate Telling You How I Really Feel* (2019) from Bloof Books. She is also the author of an artist book called "Operation USA" through the Baltimore based book arts group Container, a project acquired by Woodland Pattern Book Center in Milwaukee. Her third collection, *Waterbaby*, is forthcoming from Copper Canyon Press in 2021.

Dylan Weir is a poet and teacher, currently at Columbia College in Chicago. He earned an MFA from the University of Wisconsin–Madison, waited tables at The Bread Loaf Writer's Conference, and has poems in: *Meridian, Ninth Letter, North American Review, Passages North, Salt Hill, Sycamore Review*, and others.

Marcus Wicker is the recipient of a Ruth Lilly Fellowship from the Poetry Foundation, a Pushcart Prize, The Missouri Review's Miller Audio Prize, as well as fellowships from Cave Canem, and the Fine Arts Work Center. His first collection *Maybe the Saddest Thing* (Harper Perennial), a National Poetry Series winner, was a finalist for an NAACP Image Award. Wicker's poems have appeared in *The Nation, Poetry, American Poetry Review, Oxford American*, and *Boston Review*. His second book, *Silencer—*

also an Image Award finalist—was published by Houghton Mifflin Harcourt in 2017 and won the Society of Midland Authors Award, as well as the Arnold Adoff Poetry Award for New Voices. Marcus teaches in the MFA program at the University of Memphis, and he is the poetry editor of *Southern Indiana Review*.

Jameka Williams is an MFA candidate at Northwestern University hailing from Chester, Pennsylvania, fifteen miles southeast of Philadelphia. Her poetry has been published in *Prelude Magazine, Gigantic Sequins, Powder Keg Magazine, Jet Fuel Review, Yemassee Journal, Tupelo Quarterly,* and is forthcoming in *Painted Bride Quarterly*. Muzzle Magazine nominated her poem, "Yeezus' Wife [when asked what do you actually do]," for Best of the Net 2017 and the Pushcart Prize. She resides in Chicago, Illinois.

John Sibley Williams is the author of *As One Fire Consumes Another* (Orison Poetry Prize, 2019), *Skin Memory* (Backwaters Prize, University of Nebraska Press, 2019), *Summon* (JuxtaProse Chapbook Prize, 2019), *Disinheritance,* and *Controlled Hallucinations*. He has also served as editor of two Northwest poetry anthologies, *Alive at the Center* (Ooligan Press, 2013) and *Motionless from the Iron Bridge* (barebones books, 2013). A nineteen-time Pushcart nominee, John is the winner of numerous awards, including the Laux/Millar Prize, Wabash Prize, Philip Booth Award, Janet B. McCabe Poetry Prize, American Literary Review Poetry Contest, Phyllis Smart-Young Prize, The 46er Prize, Nancy D. Hargrove Editors' Prize, Confrontation Poetry Prize, and Vallum Award for Poetry. He serves as editor of *The Inflectionist Review* and works as a freelance poetry editor, writing coach, and literary agent. Previous publishing credits include: *Yale Review, Midwest Quarterly, Southern Review, Colorado Review, Sycamore Review, Prairie Schooner, Massachusetts Review, Poet Lore, Saranac Review, Atlanta Review, TriQuarterly, Columbia Poetry Review, Mid-American Review, Poetry Northwest, Third Coast,* and various anthologies.

Khaty Xiong hails from Fresno, California. She is the author of *Poor Anima* (Apogee Press, 2015), which holds the distinction of being the first full-length collection of poetry published by a Hmong American woman in the United States. She's held the Nadya Aisenberg Fellowship at The MacDowell Colony and an Individual Excellence Award from the Ohio Arts Council. She currently holds the 2019 Roxane Gay Fellowship in Poetry from Jack Jones Literary Arts. Her work has been published in *Poetry*, the *New York Times*, *How Do I Begin?: A Hmong American Literary Anthology* (Heyday, 2011), and elsewhere.

SERIES EDITORS

————

Rita Mae Reese coedits the anthology series *New Poetry from the Midwest*. She is the author of *The Alphabet Conspiracy* and *The Book of Hulga*, which was selected by Denise Duhamel for the Felix Pollak Prize. She is a recipient of a Rona Jaffe Foundation Writers' Award, a Stegner fellowship in fiction, a Discovery/The Nation Prize, and a Pamaunok Poetry Prize, among other awards. She is the Director of Literary Arts at the Arts + Literature Laboratory in Madison, Wisconsin. She can be found at www.ritamaereese.com.

Hannah Stephenson coedits the anthology series *New Poetry from the Midwest*. She is a poet and editor living in Columbus, Ohio (where she also runs a literary event series called Paging Columbus). She is the author of *Cadence* (which won the Ohio Chapbook Prize from the Wick Poetry Center) *and In the Kettle, the Shriek*. Her writing has appeared in *The Atlantic*, *The Huffington Post*, *32 Poems*, *The Journal*, and *Poetry Daily*. You can visit her online at http://thestorialist.com.

HEARTLAND POETRY PRIZE JUDGE

————

William Evans is a writer, instructor and performer from Columbus, OH. He founded the Writing Wrongs Poetry Slam in 2009 and appeared on seven National Slam teams from Columbus collectively. His work can be seen online in *Radius Poetry*, *The Legendary*, *Joint Literary Magazine*, and other publications.